The People's College

The People's College

Little Rock Junior College and
Little Rock University,
1927-1969

James E. Lester, Jr.

August House / Little Rock
P U B L I S H E R S

Printed in the United States of America

10 9 8 7 6 5 4 3 2 1

LIBRARY OF CONGRESS CATALOGING-IN-PUBLICATION DATA
Lester, Jim, 1945-
The people's college.

Bibliography: p.229
Includes index
1. Little Rock University — History. 2. Little Rock Junior College — History. I. Title.
LD3071.L9665.L47   1987   378.767′73   87-15179
ISBN 0-87483-052-4

First Edition, 1987

Cover illustration by Wendell E. Hall
Production artwork by Ira Hocut
Typography by Diversified Graphics, Little Rock, AR
Design direction by Ted Parkhurst
Project direction by Hope Coulter

This book is printed on archival-quality paper which meets the guidelines for
performance and durability of the Committee on Production Guidelines for Book
Longevity of the Council on Library Resources.

AUGUST HOUSE, INC.   PUBLISHERS   LITTLE ROCK

*This one
is for my mother and my brother,
who made the bad times better.*

Contents

Acknowledgments

I would like to thank the staff of the archives of the Otten-heimer Library at the University of Arkansas at Little Rock for their assistance in the preparation of this volume. For over a year, the members of the staff — Linda Pine, Joy Geisler, Rebecca Bowman, and others — cheerfully dropped whatever they happened to be doing to help me locate needed information. I also welcome the opportunity to thank Dr. Bobby Roberts, the director of the archives, who had the confidence in me to do the project. In addition, I would like to acknowledge the help I received from Diane Wilson of the UALR alumni office and the many former Little Rock Junior College and Little Rock University instructors and other personnel who shared their insights and memories of the institution with me.

James E. Lester, Jr.

Introduction

*I*n July 1929, a young woman named Mary Best wrote a thank-you note to former Arkansas Governor George W. Donaghey. The governor had recently endowed an educational experiment in Little Rock — a two-year-old junior college with approximately 100 students that met in the north wing of the local high school — and Mary Best wanted to express her appreciation to the school's new benefactor. In the letter, she told Donaghey of the anxiety she had suffered during her high school years because she knew her parents lacked the financial resources to send her away to college. "If the Junior College had not been opened the year I finished," she wrote, "I probably would be making fifteen dollars a week now with no chance of advancement." Instead, Mary had worked part-time and attended the junior college until her graduation the previous spring. She then proudly informed Governor Donaghey, "I have recently been given an appointment to teach in the Little Rock Public Schools which will enable me to continue my education and help educate my sisters. May I thank you again for this education."[1]

Forty years after Mary Best graduated from the struggling junior college, the institution became the University of Arkansas at Little Rock, offering educational opportunities to over 3000 students in a physical plant valued in excess of eight million dollars. In the interim, the school relocated, first to an old public school building at Thirteenth and State Streets and later to a spacious campus on Hayes Street (now University Avenue), and for almost a dozen years, between 1957 and 1969, functioned as Little Rock University. No matter where the institution was located or under which name it operated, its main purpose remained to provide college-level education for students like Mary Best. Although Little Rock Junior College and later Little Rock University received no public financial support until 1969, the college nevertheless offered relatively inexpensive higher education to thousands of students in central Arkansas who, for one reason or another, could not leave home to attend school. Like other junior colleges throughout the country, LRJC therefore served as a "people's college," operating with a virtual open admissions policy, offering college classes to students of all ages in the local area.

Little Rock Junior College made a difference in Mary Best's life, and that fact demonstrates why institutions of higher education play a significant role in

American culture. Whether young people attend a local junior college, a state university, or an expensive private college, during their years at that institution they will finish forming basic attitudes and values, make decisions about careers and marriage, and complete preparations for entrance into adult life. In effect, the nation's future is shaped by our colleges and universities.

In addition, those institutions serve important economic functions for the state and local communities where they are located. They provide services and facilities for business, agriculture, and government, and their faculties, along with teaching, conduct research to advance the general conditions of American life. A local college or university also produces jobs and consumes goods and services, thus becoming an economic asset to the community as a whole.

Studying the histories of these educational institutions provides perspectives that help govern future growth. Understanding the development of a school — how its fundamental mission evolved, what kind of students attended it, how it raised needed funding — enables planners to reach more enlightened and rational decisions about new directions for the institution.

Colleges and universities are also important because they contribute to the overall history of their local communities. In Little Rock, thousands of business leaders, government employees, professional people, and others received their training at LRJC, LRU, or UALR, developing common, community-based bonds that help make the Arkansas capital unique. Just as fixtures like the Arkansas River and the state capital played a part in the evolution of the city, the college also made an important contribution to the community's cultural and intellectual life.

Along with its role in the annals of the city of Little Rock, LRJC served as a microcosm of the history of the junior college movement in America. Starting in the late nineteenth century and accelerating in the 1920s, when Little Rock Junior College was founded, the junior college movement grew out of the nation's public school system and reflected an impulse to extend educational opportunities to all people regardless of social class or family income. Educator Lawrence A. Kimpton wrote that "no other element of American education is more democratic, more economical, and less badgered by false and snobbish sentimentalities" than the junior college.[2]

Despite their noble origins in egalitarianism — a value supposedly cherished by Americans — junior colleges often suffered from an image of inferiority. From the beginning of the movement the term "junior" implied a lower status, and often even junior college administrators seemed confused about whether their schools were extensions of local secondary schools or separate institutions of higher education. Individuals connected with traditional four-year colleges sometimes regarded junior colleges as havens for the stupid or the poor, and such unfair generalizations contributed to an indentity crisis in the minds of many people connected with two-year colleges.

The school in Little Rock proved especially slow in establishing a positive identity. Operating under the direction of the publicly elected Little Rock School Board for many years, LRJC seemed to be an extension of the public school program. After the mid-1930s the board gave the college more autonomy, and the faculty and administration then attempted to establish a niche as an institution of higher education separate from the city's public primary and secondary schools. Even after the college evolved into Little Rock University in 1957, school authorities had to fight an erroneous popular perception that LRU meant "Last Resort University" — an inferior institution to be attended only when all other avenues had failed. In 1969, when LRU merged with the University of Arkansas at Fayetteville, the college community again suffered a crisis of self-image and identity, as many people wondered if UALR had become merely a branch campus of the institution commonly known in Arkansas as *the* University."

Part of the Little Rock school's difficulty in establishing a positive image in the hierarchy of higher educational institutions in the state stemmed from its recent origins. In the public mind, Little Rock Junior College/Little Rock University/the University of Arkansas at Little Rock had no past, no tradition, no lineage. This volume is an effort to correct that situation. The college in Little Rock does have a past. It has served the community well for 60 years, educating and training generations of productive citizens, the majority of whom have remained in central Arkansas, contributing to the area's growth and development. Just as Little Rock Junior College made a difference in Mary Best's life, it has also made a difference in the city of Little Rock, for without the institution, the intellectual, cultural, and economic life of the community would be considerably diminished.

John A. Larson, the founder and president of Little Rock Junior College until his death in 1949.

C H A P T E R   O N E

Creating a People's College

*A*braham Lincoln once called education "the most important subject which we as a people can be engaged in," and since the days of colonial New England the American people have demonstrated an unyielding faith in the importance of educating their children. To this end, Americans have built a variety of institutions to teach their young everything from reading and writing to the principles of nuclear physics. Throughout the nation communities have erected one-room schoolhouses, million-dollar high school facilities, small liberal arts colleges, and giant universities to meet their insatiable demand for learning. In 1927 the same zeal led educators in Little Rock, Arkansas, to make an important addition to the city's school system. Hardly noticed by the press or the public at the time, Little Rock Junior College was to evolve over the next 60 years into one of the foremost institutions of higher education in the state of Arkansas.

"Jaycee," as students soon referred to the new school, resulted from the sudden termination of lower-level college courses which the University of Arkansas at Fayetteville had been offering on an extension basis in the capital city. The removal of this program generated an outcry by local students and their

parents and prompted educational and civic leaders to investigate the possibility of establishing a new institution that would offer the benefits of higher education to the people of central Arkansas.[1]

Most of the undergraduates affected by Fayetteville's decision lacked the funds to attend school away from home, and many of them held part-time or even full-time jobs while participating in the University of Arkansas program. The plan for a new college originated in the urgent appeals both of those who had taken some of the university courses and of recent high school graduates who wished to continue their education in the Little Rock area.

These two groups soon found a spokesman for their cause in John A. Larson, the principal of Little Rock Senior High School. A native of Chanute, Kansas, Larson was born of Swedish parents and did not speak English until after his fifth birthday. His later work with the schools reflected an appreciation for hard work and a regard for learning acquired during his rural Kansas boyhood.[2] Larson was graduated from Kansas State Normal School at Emporia and also earned a master's degree from the University of Chicago. He arrived in Little Rock in 1912 to teach in the high school and became principal five years later. In the first decade of his administration he built the school into an outstanding institution and won the respect of the Little Rock community as an energetic, no-nonsense educational leader.

When several parents sought Larson's advice about the cancellation of local university classes, he became convinced that the same courses could be taught under the auspices of the Little Rock School District. Upon presenting his idea to School Superintendent R.C. Hall and the Little Rock School Board, however, Larson received a less than enthusiastic response. The members of the board felt the project might prove too expensive and discouraged him from pursuing the idea.[3] Larson ignored these initial rebuffs and continued to rally support for his dream, which had expanded from offering a few classes to creating a quality junior college in Little Rock. One early Jaycee teacher recalled that "without John Larson there never would have been a school here."[4]

Part of the explanation for Larson's success lay in his understanding of the junior college movement that had been gaining momentum in the United States since the turn of the century. Larson understood that the junior college movement was an outgrowth of the American people's faith in universal education. Originating with the early Puritan settlers who wanted literate church members and consequently established schools in every township in New England, the high value placed on education grew under the reform spirit of the Jacksonian era. By the 1860s, after the Civil War, it developed into a movement for free public high schools. In the landmark *Kalamazoo* decision of 1872, the United States Supreme Court established a significant precedent in the history of public education by ruling that public high schools in Michigan should receive support from public taxation.[5] This principle of tax-supported secondary education was the first vital step in the junior college movement, for "people's colleges" would later evolve from local public high schools.

Besides the structure of tax support for schools, the availability of vocational training in education also became an issue. The Morrill Act of 1862 established land grants for colleges to train students in agriculture and the mechanical arts — schools embodying several basic ideas that later became the foundation of the junior college movement. For example, they offered low-cost education to young people from families of average means and provided a non-classical curriculum designed to give students practical, vocational training. In addition, they established an important model for federal support of higher education.[6]

Although the various colleges and state universities created by the Morrill Act did extend educational opportunities to young people from less affluent backgrounds, the cost of tuition plus the expenses of living away from home still prevented some students from acquiring needed training beyond high school. As a result, by the beginning of the new century a movement in support of a unique educational institution gained momentum.[7]

This demand coincided with a trend in American higher education to emulate the university system used in Germany. In the mid-nineteenth century, many American scholars completing their graduate work at German universities had come to admire the German method of separating the first two years of college work, which they regarded as essentially preparatory, from the later years, which offered more specialized training. As these American scholars — many of them educators — reached positions of influence in the latter part of the century, they recommended that the first two years of collegiate work either be transferred to the secondary schools or be done in separate academies devoted solely to preparatory education.

Responding to this impulse, William R. Harper, president of the University of Chicago, in 1892 introduced a plan to affiliate a number of small colleges with his university by accepting their work as equivalent to that offered by the University of Chicago through the sophomore year. Later called the "father of the junior college," Harper hoped eventually to eliminate the freshman and sophomore years at Chicago so that the university could concentrate on more advanced studies. In a speech delivered in 1900, Harper said that "the work of the Freshman and Sophomore years is only a continuation of the Academy or high school work. It is a continuation not only of subject matter but of the methods employed."[8] Harper suggested that junior colleges could be created by limiting weak four-year schools to only two years of college work, building new two-year institutions, or adding two years of work to existing high school programs — and it was this upward extension of secondary schools that proved to be the most widely adopted method in the creation of junior colleges after the turn of the century.

Harper helped create a pair of private junior colleges in the Chicago area — Lewis Institute in 1896 and Bradley Institute in Peoria in 1897 — and in 1901 influenced the establishment of a public junior college in Joliet. Although the institution at Joliet claimed to be America's first public junior college, school officials in Greeley, Colorado, and Saginaw, Michigan, also made similar claims.[9] Building on Harper's efforts in Illinois, the junior college movement entered a formative period over the next 20 years. The number of junior colleges grew slowly until the 1920s, when a sharp increase in the construction of new two-year institutions, including Little Rock Junior College, resulted from the prosperity of the post-World War I era.[10]

California was the first state to authorize the establishment of junior or community colleges. In 1907 the California legislature passed a law allowing local boards of education to provide the first two years of college work, and in 1910 Fresno became the first California city to establish a public junior college. In 1921 the legislature created independent districts; by 1930, the state had over 15,000 students enrolled in 345 recently created two-year institutions.[11]

The popularity of the early junior colleges, both in California and throughout the nation, came from several sources. Often referred to as "workingman's colleges" or "people's colleges," these institutions appealed to families whose financial circumstances prevented them from sending their children away to school but who wanted their offspring to "join the white-collar and professional ranks."[12] These largely lower-middle-class families reflected Americans' faith in education as the key to upward mobility. They saw the newly emerging junior colleges as a unique chance to equalize educational opportunities, since the new schools generally kept tuition rates low and allowed students to continue living at home, often while working at part-time jobs.

The junior colleges also made higher education possible for undergraduates who were unprepared academically or emotionally to enter more established four-year institutions.[13] Some students tended to be too immature for university life away from home, and by the 1920s educators recognized that in these cases delaying the separation from home by one or two years often meant the difference in academic success and failure.[14] The new two-year institutions also kept young people out of the job market for a while and then furnished the marketplace with more mature and better trained individuals than those with only a high school diploma.

The appeal of junior colleges increased between 1920 and 1940 as the schools underwent a period of diversification, during which they broadened their curricula to include vocational and adult educational programs. These years also witnessed the rapid growth of new junior colleges, as publicly supported institutions supplanted private two-year schools.

In 1922, at the beginning of this era, representatives of American two-year colleges held a national convention and adopted an official definition of a junior college as "an institution offering two years of strictly collegiate grade."[15] By 1925 these leaders recognized that changing circumstances demanded an enlargement of their earlier definition. Under the new designation a junior college would offer courses identical to the

corresponding ones in a standard four-year institution, and in addition could develop "a different type of curriculum suited to the larger and ever-changing civic, social, religious, and vocational needs of the entire community ...."[16] This concept of community service became an important part of the junior college movement and proved to be especially important at the institution created by John Larson in Little Rock in 1927.

The establishment of the Little Rock school corresponded to the general increase in the number of two-year institutions throughout the country. In Texas, for example, seventeen school systems established junior college programs between 1922 and 1929. In 1927, the year Larson founded Little Rock Junior College, school authorities created 32 new junior colleges throughout the country, and by 1936 enrollments in junior colleges represented seventeen percent of all undergraduates in the arts and sciences.[17] In 1900 the United States had only 8 junior colleges serving approximately 100 students, but, as a result of the increased popularity of the movement, by 1950 more than 600 two-year institutions had a combined student population of over 500,000.[18]

This phenomenal growth represented what one historian called the "most significant contribution which our nation has made to the entire history of education."[19] Resulting from nineteenth-century efforts to reform American universities, then gaining momentum from increased interest in adult and vocational education to meet the needs of an industrialized society, the junior college movement fused with a general tendency toward the democratization of the educational process that has characterized American education in the twentieth century.

That same democratic faith marked the spread of junior colleges in Arkansas. The founders of these institutions wanted to serve young people who were unable to afford the cost of higher education at distant colleges and universities, and the two-year schools that survived and expanded became an important part of the history of higher education in the state.

Educators in Arkansas established at least 20 junior colleges in the early twentieth century. Some of these institutions had church affiliations, while others were either proprietary schools, public schools, or municipal junior colleges. Crescent College at Eureka Springs became the first junior college in the state in 1908, when officials decided to continue the work started by Maddox Seminary in Little Rock on a limited basis in northwest Arkansas. Between 1908 and its closure in 1934, Crescent College served as a junior college for girls, emphasizing music, literature, and teacher certification to a student body that remained stable at around 100 women. During the summer months the school building served as a resort hotel to help raise money for the institution. Contemporary observers regarded Crescent College as a "high class school for its time."[20]

Although Crescent College was the first junior college in the state, the creation of four district agricultural schools proved to be of far greater importance to the history of higher education in Arkansas. The idea for separate agricultural schools originated with the Washington County Farmers' Union, which

launched a lobbying effort to create the institutions in 1906. The "farmers' schools" caught the imagination of Governor George Donaghey, who later played a pivotal role in the establishment of Little Rock Junior College, and under his leadership in April 1909 the state legislature passed a bill creating four institutions that would offer high school work along with vocational training. Located in Jonesboro, Russellville, Magnolia, and Monticello, the schools all evolved from their agricultural beginnings into first junior colleges, then four-year institutions, and finally universities: Arkansas State University (Jonesboro); Arkansas Tech University (Russellville); Southern Arkansas University (Magnolia); and the University of Arkansas at Monticello.

The concept of a junior college also appealed to Arkansas's religious educators. State Methodist leaders operated Galloway Women's College at Searcy as a two-year school for a brief time, and starting in 1919 various Arkansas Baptist groups established and operated small junior colleges at Jonesboro, Mountain Home, Sheridan, Pocahontas, Walnut Ridge, and Conway. During these early years, educators tended to use terms like "school," "college," and "academy" interchangeably, and the exact status of some of these institutions remains rather vague.[21]

This difficulty of definition marked the two leading proprietary junior colleges created in the state in the first quarter of the century. Established in Little Rock in 1900 by John F. Draughon of Nashville, Tennessee, Draughon's School of Business trained young people for commercial careers, and while it was never a junior college in the usual sense of the term, the school belonged to the American Association of Junior Colleges until 1951.[22] A second proprietary school grew out of the efforts of John E. Brown, an evangelist and lecturer who founded Southwestern Collegiate Institute at Siloam Springs in 1919. Offering a largely practical curriculum, the school required vocational work by all students. SCI evolved into John Brown University and by maintaining its vocational requirements remained one of the most unusual institutions of higher education in the state.

Several Arkansas municipalities also became enamored with the junior college movement in the 1920s. For example, the El Dorado School Board founded El Dorado Junior College in 1925 with only 23 students. Although the institution flourished for a few years, local officials discontinued it in 1942, primarily because of a lack of funding.[23]

Three years after the opening of El Dorado Junior College, school officials in Fort Smith began conducting college classes in the local high school building. Starting with 128 students, Fort Smith Junior College offered standard freshman- and sophomore-level courses, along with vocational training for stenographers, bookkeepers, secretaries, and clerks. In the late 1930s, the school board expanded FSJC's vocational curriculum to include training in automobile mechanics, drafting, woodworking, and pottery. Educational leaders in Hot Springs also attempted to establish a junior college in their community in 1940, but poor planning and inadequate funds forced Hot Springs Junior College to close after only two years of operation.

Dunbar Junior College, located at Wright Avenue and Ringo Street in Little Rock, was for years the only junior college in the state open to black students. Organized in 1929 as an extension of Dunbar High School, the college offered programs in home economics, teacher education, and the liberal arts. It received generous grants from the Rosenwald Fund and the General Education Board; by 1954, three-fourths of the black teachers in the capital city had received their basic training at Dunbar. The Little Rock School Board acted as a board of trustees, and the principal of Dunbar High School served as the administrative head of the junior college.[24]

The same administrative structure provided the basic governance system for the largest and one of the most important two-year schools in Arkansas — Little Rock Junior College. Established in 1927 under the guiding hand of John Larson, LRJC represented a renewed effort by the Little Rock community both to improve the city's secondary schools and to furnish the young people of the capital with at least a semblance of higher education.

The city had had a college as early as the 1850s when the Grand Lodge of the Arkansas Masons established St. John's College, but the Civil War ended the school's brief career and forced local educators to concentrate on providing primary and secondary schooling. By 1869 the Little Rock School District offered eight years of instruction to all students; that same year city officials opened the town's first high school at Eighth and Sherman Streets. Throughout the remainder of the nineteenth century the citizens of Little Rock did not exhibit much zeal for higher education, and in August 1871 they rejected a bond issue to finance the proposed Arkansas Industrial University. The institution eventually found a home in the northwest Arkansas city of Fayetteville, and later became the University of Arkansas.

In the meantime, the Freedmen's Aid Society of the Northern Methodist Church opened Little Rock University in the capital city in 1882. Originally located between Fourth and Fifth Streets on the east side of Main Street, the school, because of its association with the unpopular Freedman's Aid Society, never had the support of the community and folded after a few years.[25] Over the ensuing decades several other small and unsuccessful colleges also opened and closed in Little Rock, leaving the capital city without a major institution of higher education.

By 1927 the city had a population of over 95,000 and an excellent system of public education — at least for white students — but citizens' support for advanced education was still minimal. However, the popularity of the junior college movement, the general prosperity of the 1920s, and the personality of John Larson finally combined to create a collegiate institution that would have a lasting impact on the city.

Before the founding of Little Rock Junior College, high school graduates in central Arkansas who wished to continue their education while living at home had only the option of the limited number of extension courses offered through the University of Arkansas at Fayetteville. Starting in 1923, the extension system utilized secondary teachers who held master's degrees and conducted classes in the late afternoon and evening in the high school building at Fourteenth and Scott Streets. By 1926 the University

Extension Service offered one full year of college work that included a teacher training course, but university officials deemed the Little Rock experiment economically unsound and cancelled the program in the spring of 1927.

Responding to the demands of students and parents to fill the sudden vacuum in higher education in the Little Rock area, John Larson organized his junior college project. Proposing that high school teachers with master's degrees could be used on a part-time basis, he convinced the Little Rock School Board that tuition from the students in each class would be sufficient to cover the initial expenses of the school.[26]

Throughout the summer of 1927 Larson contacted every student who had taken the University of Arkansas extension courses the previous year and explained how the new junior college would operate. He also recruited new students from the 1927 graduating class of Little Rock Senior High School.

The success of Larson's plan hinged on the availability of classroom space in the city's new high school building, which opened in September 1927 at Fourteenth and Park. The $1.5 million facility received national recognition as one of the largest and most attractive high schools in the United States,[27] and included over 100 classrooms with the capacity to seat more than 3000 students. Since the student body in the high school numbered considerably less than that, Larson proposed to the board that a set of rooms on the second floor of the north end of the building be reserved for classes for the proposed junior college.

Although Larson's persistence finally convinced the school board to approve

Little Rock Central High School, formerly Little Rock Senior High School, where the first classes of Little Rock Junior College met in 1927. (Arkansas History Commission)

the project, board members insisted that the Little Rock School District would in no way assume any financial responsibility for the junior college. The board designated Larson as dean of the college without compensation and maintained that the school would have to be self-supporting from revenues raised through tuition. However, it did agree not to make the new college pay for lighting, heating, water, or janitorial service.[28] In September 1927 Little Rock Junior College officials registered its first students in a standard two-year liberal arts program. School Superintendent R.C. Hall served as president of the new junior college. The school's faculty consisted of only one full-time teacher, Lula B. Chase, who taught psychology and coordinated the teacher training program, and a group of part-time instructors who also taught in the high school — J.H. Atkinson, history and economics; J.A. Bigbee, mathematics; Dorothy Yarnell, English; Pauline

Hoeltzel, German; Florence Beltz, Spanish; and Mary Murphy, French.

The first student body had approximately 100 members who paid $5 per semester-hour in tuition in addition to a small library fee. Most of them had graduated from high school in the spring of 1927, although between 20 and 30 students had either taken the University of Arkansas extension courses or had previously attended college elsewhere.[29]

In almost every respect, the new Little Rock Junior College reflected the typical organizational pattern of junior colleges established nationwide in the 1920s. One later authority on the history of the junior college movement described the usual pattern followed in the creation of a junior college — a model that fit LRJC perfectly. "In the early days," Professor Charles R. Monroe wrote, "the junior college was typically housed in a portion of the local high school building ... The school principal was the dean of the col-

R.C. Hall, president of the Little Rock
School Board and the first president of Little
Rock Junior College.

lege and the superintendent of the public schools served as the president of the college."[30]

The new institution in Little Rock also offered typical inducements to recruit students. One early LRJC *Bulletin* advised prospective enrollees that "the Junior College offers peculiar advantages both to the students who cannot afford to live away from home and to the young and immature students who are not ready to cope with the problems of college life."[31] LRJC literature also promised that the institution would be less expensive than colleges outside the Little Rock area and that its smaller classes offered more individual attention. Finally, Jaycee authorities made an appeal that would remain a hallmark of student recruitment at the Little Rock college for over half a century, arguing that students would be more likely to secure part-time employment in the capital city than in a smaller community.

Despite these advantages, students who attended Little Rock Junior College during the school's first few years of operation took an educational risk. Many small colleges, conceived with the same good intentions, failed to survive once initial enthusiasm waned under the pressures of financial and other difficulties. Even the Little Rock School Board warned that "the pupils who take the course are advised that there is no guarantee that their credits will be accepted at full value...."[32] The first students who enrolled in the fledgling institution placed their confidence in a new concept of higher education and the dreams of John A. Larson. The early years of the school's existence consequently provided a stern test of Little Rock's newest experiment in advanced learning.

Arkansas Governor George W. Donaghey, whose generous endowment in 1929 gave LRJC a solid financial foundation for over 40 years.

LRJC at Work and Play, 1927-1931

*F*or two years, John Larson's experiment in higher education endured solely supported by income from tuition and fees. Even though the school had limited funds and relied on the charity of the Little Rock School District, parents and students had faith that Larson would find additional revenue to enable the college to survive and eventually to expand. And two years after its founding, Little Rock Junior College did receive a significant gift that not only insured the school's continued existence but also renewed the hope of the community that someday Little Rock would have a quality institution of higher learning.

On July 1, 1929, LRJC became the sole beneficiary of a trust established by former Arkansas governor George W. Donaghey and his wife. Valued in excess of $2,000,000, Donaghey's bequest was the largest single donation to an Arkansas institution up to that time.[1] It involved perpetual increments from two of Little Rock's finest office buildings, both located at Seventh and Main — the Donaghey Building (then the tallest office building in the city) and the Federal Bank and Trust Building. Donaghey also appointed a board of trustees, including G. DeMatt Henderson, J.F. Loughborough, Alfred G. Kahn, F.W. Niemeyer, Charles L. Thompson, Leo Pfeifer, and Fred W. Allsopp, to administer the endowment, who along with other Donaghey trustees played a major role in the growth of the college over the ensuing decades. Donaghey was 73 the day he executed his bequest; this act of generosity marked the high point of a career devoted to various progressive causes, especially those involving education in Arkansas.

Donaghey had attended the University of Arkansas in Fayetteville in 1882-83 before moving to Conway, where he worked as a contractor and developed a reputation as a local political figure, running unsuccessfully as a Prohibition candidate for mayor in 1885.[2] In 1899 he received an appointment to the commission in charge of erecting the new state capitol in Little Rock. Because of construction delays, Donaghey made the completion of the building the cornerstone of his successful gubernatorial campaign in 1908. Reelected in 1910, the governor fulfilled his promise despite charges of corruption stemming from the construction of the capitol, and the state legislature met in the new structure for the first time in 1911.

During his years as the governor of Arkansas, Donaghey became part of the Progressive movement that influenced American political life in the era of Theodore Roosevelt and Woodrow Wilson.

The Arkansas governor promoted the adoption of the initiative and referendum procedures, supported numerous public health programs, and fought against Arkansas's notorious convict-lease system, under which the state rented prisoners to private contractors for small sums of money. Commenting that the convicts lived in "burning, seething Hells," Donaghey granted 360 pardons to inmates he judged to be serving long sentences for minor offenses, and thereby ruined the corrupt leasing system.[3]

Although defeated for a third term in 1912, Donaghey continued to further progressive causes after leaving the state-house while continuing his successful career as a builder. Many reforms he supported involved improvements in Arkansas's educational system. Having earlier helped secure Hendrix College, Central College, and the State Normal School for Conway, he actively promoted public primary and secondary education as well as the establishment of the four state agricultural colleges during his term as the state's chief executive. After leaving the governor's office, he acted as chairman of Governor Thomas McRae's Education Commission in 1921 and served for many years as chairman of the Board of Trustees of Philander Smith College, a private all-black school in Little Rock.[4]

Donaghey and his wife, the former Louvenia Wallace of Lonoke County, never had any children of their own and, according to the former governor, fell "into the habit of calling all the young people of Arkansas our children."[5] For several years the couple talked about bequeathing the bulk of their estate to "some Arkansas school," but by the late 1920s the ex-governor had become more specific. "After frequent consultations with the school authorities," Donaghey later wrote, "I was convinced that no greater field for educational development exists anywhere than can be found right here in Little Rock, where hundreds of boys and girls, after graduating from high school, are unable to advance further through a course in college."[6] In an interview conducted several years after the establishment of the trust, Mrs. Donaghey added that she and her husband "felt that a junior college in Little Rock had definite possibilities for growing larger, so we decided to endow it."[7]

This optimism regarding the future of the school prevailed among the supporters of the junior college following the announcement of the Donaghey gift. "The significance of the Donaghey endowment is wide," one student editor wrote. "It means that tens of thousands of boys and girls in the years to come will enjoy higher educational advantages that would otherwise be beyond their reach."[8] An instructor at the college pointed out that the Donaghey gift focused statewide attention on the fledgling institution and noted that it was "quite remarkable" that the largest private college endowment in the state had been created for an institution only two years old.[9]

Initially, the Donaghey endowment seemed to fuel only faith in the future of Little Rock Junior College. For the first few years, while the income from the buildings went toward liquidating the indebtedness on the property, the college received an average of less than $3000 a year from the Donaghey Foundation, and had to continue to operate primarily on money from tuition payments.

Despite the initially meager income, the establishment of the Donaghey Foundation gave the supporters of LRJC a feeling their college would endure. The former governor and his wife called the institution "Junior" and often referred to Jaycee as their "child."[10] They hoped "Junior" would grow and prosper and, in a speech delivered only a few years after establishing the trust, Donaghey expressed his hope for the future of Little Rock Junior College. "When fifty years have passed," he said, "and a great university is sending out its thousands of young men and women to bless humanity ... I [would] like to think that with the endowment I have been able to give, my life has not been in vain."[11]

While the efforts of John Larson and George Donaghey created a solid foundation for Little Rock Junior College, the work of the faculty and students enabled the school to grow substantially between 1927 and 1931. In the spring of 1929, after less than two years of existence, Jaycee received full accreditation from the North Central Association of Colleges and Secondary Schools. Before the school's accreditation, students had feared that their time and effort might be in some sense wasted, and consequently, as the student newspaper reported, "[W]hen the news came through that LRJC had been accredited by North Central, all the school was wildly happy ...."[12]

The accrediting and the announcement of the Donaghey endowment in the summer of 1929 removed any doubts about the college in the eyes of the Little Rock community, to the point that the 1929 fall enrollment jumped to 347 students from only 119 the previous year.[13] Apparently John Larson's assessment of the need for an institution of higher learning in the capital city had been accurate.

Larson and others connected with the school also correctly perceived that prospective students in the area wanted an institution that emphasized basic preparatory college work. During the boom in junior college building in the 1920s, supporters of the movement had become divided over the function of a junior college. While one group maintained that a junior college should prepare students for advanced work in the university or at least give them the fundamentals of a liberal arts education, other educators maintained that the new two-year schools should stress vocational training and not simply try to duplicate what older, four-year institutions were already doing. This latter group contended that most early colleges in America had been essentially vocational — established to supply trained clergymen for the colonies — and that the new junior colleges should return to that principle and stress occupational training in areas like bookkeeping, secretarial work, cosmetology, carpentry, welding, and automobile mechanics.

From the beginning, the administrators of Little Rock Junior College rejected a primary emphasis on vocational training. Although several years later school leaders did expand the curriculum to include occupational training courses, Jaycee's main focus remained traditional college work. As early as 1930, the *Bulletin* of the school defined the purpose of the institution accordingly: "[F]irst, it offers two years of general college work. Second it offers ... prerequisites for entrance to the professional school. Third, it provides two years of specialized education as the teacher's training and commerce and finance curricula."[14] The general college work referred to in the *Bulletin* included two years of English, two years of a foreign language, one year each of history and mathematics, eight hours of laboratory science, and fourteen to eighteen hours of elective courses. In the 1920s and 1930s the pre-professional work offered by Jaycee proved to be especially important. Medical, dental, and law schools required only two years of basic collegiate studies for admission, and Little Rock Junior College offered a complete pre-professional program in these areas "so that students are well equipped to do the work of professional and technical schools."[15] The college offered an Associate of Arts degree and required completion of 60 hours of academic work and 4 hours of physical education or hygiene, with no more than 40 hours carried in the freshman year in order to graduate.

In the fall of 1929, school officials added late afternoon and evening classes to the junior college's program, initially to accommodate local school teachers who wanted to obtain advanced credit.[16] That year 145 students enrolled in the evening classes, and in ensuing decades the night school program at LRJC became one of the most important aspects of Little Rock's "people's college."

To augment the work of both day students and those who attended evening classes, the administration created a college library in the fall of 1927. Larson borrowed books from the high school library, instructors loaned volumes from their personal collections, and the faculty solicited donations from the citizens of Little Rock. At the end of the first year of operation the Jaycee library contained 1430 volumes.[17] Before a second-floor classroom was converted for the purpose, Larson housed the library in an unused storeroom. Lack of funds prevented hiring a full-time librarian the first year, and

several students divided the tasks of record-keeping and administering the library, but during the second year the school hired Phyllis Perkins as Little Rock Junior College's first regular librarian.[18]

At the conclusion of the spring semester in 1928, twelve students who had previous college work before attending the new school were graduated from Little Rock Junior College in a combined ceremony with the Little Rock High School graduation exercises. The first graduates included Justus Matlock, Granville Davis, Thelma Williams, Martha Manees, Julia Manees, Mrs. Theo Speirs, Mary Lee Byrd, Josephine Pace, Mary Frances Elliott, June Nordman, Mary Lois Connelly, and Mary Elizabeth Middleton.

The students who attended Jaycee during that first year and throughout the late 1920s not only took pride in being a part of a bold experiment but also felt they received a quality education from the new school. One early graduate recalled that "the training I received was so thorough and so advanced that when I entered Northwestern I taught the girls in my house how to write term papers, as not one of them knew how."[19] The first undergraduates who attended LRJC also felt a unique sense of responsibility. "We knew that whether or not a college was established here depended entirely upon the work that we did," one of the early students wrote, "and we worked earnestly."[20]

These people also made every effort to make their institution a real college. From the beginning, the faculty and the students tried to establish the extracurricular trappings of collegiate life that had become so prevalent in the decade of the Roaring Twenties. For example, in October 1928 the inaugural issue of a campus newspaper appeared at Jaycee. A double column sheet, six by eight inches with six pages, the weekly paper sold for two cents a copy, with the proceeds from sales going toward the purchase of additional books for the library. Following a contest among the students, Eula Roberts won an ice cream soda for suggesting the name *College Chatter* for the newspaper. Dan Miller served as the first editor, and another student, Glen Nordin, furnished the labor and materials to print the *Chatter*.[21] The early editions of the Jaycee paper contained collegiate humor, high school news, admonitions to study hard, short stories, and editorials chastising the students for a lack of school spirit. For several years Helen Hall, a graduate of the University of Missouri School of Journalism and a part-time teacher at Jaycee, advised the students in publishing the *College Chatter*. According to J.H. Atkinson, one of the original faculty members, the *Chatter* under Hall's direction "became one of the most active agents in building the college. It gave prominence to student affairs and made faculty and students realize what was going on and what should be undertaken."[22]

In the spring of 1930 the Jaycee students added another publication to a growing list of campus institutions — the school's first yearbook, a paperback annual called the *Trojan* which sold for 50 cents a copy. Appropriately, the editors dedicated the inaugural edition of the *Trojan* to Governor and Mrs. Donaghey.[23]

In the first few years of Little Rock Junior College's existence the undergraduates formed numerous clubs and associations, many of which survived as long as the institution remained a junior college. In the late twenties some of the students and instructors organized a student council, including freshmen and sophomore class officers and elected representatives from each class, which met twice a month with a faculty committee. Like most collegiate governing bodies of the era, however, the LRJC student council had little actual voice in governing the institution.

A more significant organization was the Alpha Alpha chapter of Phi Theta Kappa, the national honorary society for junior colleges, organized by John Larson upon his return from a meeting of the American Association of Junior Colleges in November 1929. The LRJC chapter promoted both scholarship and social activities on campus, and later furnished several officers for the national organization. The charter members of the Alpha Alpha chapter included Christina Koch, Elton Carpenter, George McLaughlin, J.K. Eaker, and Mary Burt Brooks. Blanche Martin of the mathematics department served as the first faculty sponsor; beginning in 1931, Pauline Hoeltzel of the English department assumed the sponsorship, a position she held for over 25 years.[24]

In 1928 a group of coeds formed the YWCA, the first women's organization at LRJC, to offer female students the opportunities that the campus YMCA afforded the men. That same year some undergraduates with an interest in music organized the Little Rock Junior College Glee Club, and the following year the Jaycee Masquers, a dramatics club and debating society, became a part of the extracurricular activities available at the college.

Besides creating various clubs and academic organizations, the students and faculty inaugurated events that became continuing traditions throughout the life of the institution. In March 1930, for example, school officials launched "Donaghey Week" around the slogan "Honor to Whom Honor is Due." Established to pay tribute to the ex-governor for his generous endowment, the first Donaghey Week included a box supper, a series of radio programs, special editions of the campus paper, and a luncheon honoring Mr. and Mrs. Donaghey. Although the format of the celebration varied over the years, Donaghey Week remained an important campus event for almost three decades.

Student leaders also pressed for the formation of a football team. The 1920s had been a golden age of college football — the era of stars like Red Grange of Illinois and highly visible coaches like Knute Rockne of Notre Dame — and the legitimacy of a collegiate institution seemed closely tied to the prowess of the school's gridiron squad. As early as October 1929 the editor of the *Chatter* lamented that "LRJC, possessor of the largest Freshman class of any college in Arkansas, with the exception of the University, has no football team. There will be no memories of gallant teams ... no gridiron heroes ... and no sweet remembrances of hard-fought battles ..."[25]

The following year school officials remedied this situation by organizing Little Rock Junior College's first football team. Coached by Kenneth Bird, a chemistry instructor, and Johnny Estrada, a college football player just out of school, the fourteen-man squad competed against schools like Monticello A&M, Fort Smith Junior College, and El Dorado Junior College. The team played home games at Kavanaugh Field near the high school. According to the *College Chatter*, players selected the name "Trojans," which remained the designation of the school's athletic teams

for at least the next half-century.[26]

The initial Trojan football team lost all six of its games and failed to score a point throughout the entire season. Jaycee fielded teams for four more years, but school officials then abandoned the sport for over a decade because it proved to be a financial liability.[27] When the Trojans returned to the gridiron, however, the team would be considerably more successful than the inaugural LRJC squad.

A year before the formation of the football team, the school entered a men's basketball team called the Jassacks in the local city league, but the administration disbanded the squad with the season only half over.[28] The next year an LRJC basketball team competed against a number of high school and independent teams, and during the 1930-31 season John Larson, who by then was president of the college, coached the Trojan roundballers to a moderately successful season against opponents ranging from Catholic High School and Capital City Business College to a squad from the state mental hospital.[29] In the spring of 1930, the new junior college also fielded a track team called the "Trojan Warhorses"; a men's tennis team, which made a creditable showing in the state collegiate tournament; and a women's basketball team that finished second in the local YWCA league.

While these teams bore the colors of Little Rock Junior College, the selection of those colors caused one of the early controversies at the school. The *College Chatter* reported that on May 4, 1928, in an election conducted among the student body to select the official school colors, a combination of green and white won by a close margin over pink and brown. The following day the administration rejected the green and white color scheme and the

1928 junior college diplomas featured the black and gold of Little Rock Senior High School.[30] Over the next few years, the Jaycee athletic teams began wearing variations of red, crimson, or maroon and white, the last of which eventually achieved recognition as the official school colors.

Although sports never played a dominant role in student life at LRJC in the late 1920s and early 1930s, the undergraduates nevertheless exhibited a cohesiveness of the sort later called "school spirit." One alumna recalled that during her days at Jaycee in 1927-28 "there were no cliques in the school, we were just one big organization and our social affairs were entirely of the group."[31] This sense of unity stemmed from the autonomous nature of the LRJC students. The all-white student body came to junior college, with few exceptions, from local high schools. The students had known each other since childhood, and since the college had no dormitories collegiate social life often continued in the same patterns that had developed during secondary school.

Unburdened with supervising dormitory life, the LRJC faculty and administration only occasionally attempted to regulate students' behavior. In February 1929 school officials, responding to student requests, established a "social room" on the second floor of the high school, where the Jaycee classes met. Students donated magazines and furniture and raised money to purchase new drapes for the recreation center. The next fall, however, Larson, in a rare instance of administrative disciplinary action, ordered the room locked for several months. Faculty complaints of excessive noise and poor housekeeping outweighed student arguments that a social room constituted a

necessary part of college life.[32]

The controversy over the closing of the social room was a microcosm of one of the most difficult dilemmas that faced Little Rock Junior College in the school's embryonic years: the question of whether a junior college should be regarded as an extension of a secondary school program or as a separate institution of higher education. Throughout the nation in the 1920s, leaders of the new two-year schools struggled to find an adequate answer to this question and to reach a workable definition of their institutions' place in America's educational hierarchy.

Many institutions, including LRJC, found this problem compounded by the fact that the junior college had to share facilities with the local high school. One of the original teachers at Jaycee later recalled that "it was hard to distinguish high school from Jaycee students. It was against the rules for high school girls to wear silk stockings to school, but this was not the case for college girls. Sometimes a college girl with silk stockings would be stopped by a high school teacher and told to go change her stockings."[33] As late as 1930, the administration prohibited junior college students from spending their free periods or time before or after school "loitering" in the building.[34] Junior college instructors maintained daily attendance records and reported unexcused absences to the students' parents. Clearly this type of regimented routine indicated an informal definition of the college as the upper echelon of the secondary school.

This confusion extended to the local citizens. Another Little Rock Junior College instructor remembered that "for many years the community considered us an extended high school. For a while people would say to me, 'Oh, you teach in

the junior high school,' and I'd say, 'No,
I teach in the junior college.' It took
a number of years for the community to
realize that we really had two years of
accredited college work right here in
town."[35]

Like other two-year institutions
throughout the nation, LRJC suffered
from the erroneous designation of being
a "junior" college. In reality the school
was not junior to anything. Little Rock
Junior College existed as a separate,
degree-granting institution. This terminol-
ogy also contributed to the idea that
a two-year school existed simply as an inferior imitation of a regular liberal arts college, a second-rate institution catering to
undergraduates incapable of intellectual
achievement at a "senior" college. While
unquestionably some students who attended Jaycee lacked intellectual ability
and motivation, others used their education from LRJC as a foundation for
success in more prestigious four-year institutions as well as in various occu-
pations.

Soon after the inception of the college,
the faculty, administration, and students
began working to define Jaycee as a separate and strictly collegiate institution. To
make that definition workable and to help
solve the school's identity problem, John
Larson and others connected with LRJC
recognized the need for a separate campus. Consequently, after only three years
of sharing a building with Little Rock Senior High School, the junior college
sought a new image in a new location.

The campus at Thirteenth and State Streets, where LRJC was housed from 1931 to 1949.

C H A P T E R T H R E E

Beginning Again, 1931-1935

Little Rock Junior College succeeded in the school's first few years primarily because of the confidence that students, parents, and community leaders placed in John Larson. J.H. Atkinson, a long-time instructor at the institution, recalled, "Larson's enthusiasm was caught up by the students. Despite many skeptics they came to feel that students and faculty were building a college that would one day make a great place for itself in the educational world."[1] Supporters of the school maintained that faith in Larson's judgment when he recommended that the Little Rock School Board relocate the college to a separate campus. As early as the summer of 1930, the board had required that separate records and bank accounts be maintained for the high school and the junior college,[2] and by the following year board members recognized that Jaycee could never mature so long as the institution remained confined in the north wing of the high school building. In addition, Larson, as principal of Little Rock Senior High School, knew that in a few years the secondary school would need the classrooms in the north end as its own student population expanded.

Under the board's direction, Larson investigated various sites for the new campus and finally narrowed the alternatives to the upper two floors of the Donaghey Building at Seventh and Main — whose top two floors were vacant, due to a reduced demand for office space during the Depression — or the building that housed the U.M. Rose grade school at Thirteenth and State. Atkinson and John G. Pipkin, a school district official, visited both locations, examined them in detail, and reported their findings to Larson and the board. They thought that the problem of parking space in the downtown area and the possibility of having to move the school again when the economy improved made the Donaghey Building less desirable than Larson had originally thought.[3] Furthermore, they preferred the attractive site of the Rose School — a two-story building surrounded by elm trees — and appreciated the fact that the structure had originally been designed for educational purposes, and thus might suit their needs better. In a later memoir Atkinson recalled that "because of the growth of the colored population in that area, the U.M. Rose School had come to have only a small number of students and very few teachers. It was felt that it could be easily abandoned for public school purposes."[4]

As a result of Atkinson and Pipkin's

E.Q. Brothers, dean of the college for over 25 years, who also served twice as acting president.

recommendation, on March 30, 1931, the Little Rock School Board passed a motion to move Little Rock Junior College to new quarters at Thirteenth and State beginning with the fall term in September.[5] School officials spent almost $10,000 in remodeling and equipping the new junior college facility, and for the first time the college had to pay utility bills and rent — $50 a month.[6]

In September 1931, 425 students enrolled at Little Rock Junior College to attend classes in the building that would serve as Jaycee's home for the next eighteen years. During that inaugural year at the new site, administrators established a tearoom, which at the suggestion of student council president Wilbur Herring soon became known as the "Chatter Grill." Located in the southeast corner of the basement, the Grill used student help and contributed all net profits to a scholarship fund to help LRJC students.[7] For almost two decades the Chatter Grill provided undergraduates with a low-priced eating establishment as well as a gathering place to share time with their friends between classes.

Over the years, the junior college facility underwent almost constant remodeling and expansion: school officials later added a gymnasium-auditorium, the women faculty's restroom eventually became a consultation room for the dean, and a two-story frame house on nearby Izard Street became the home of the Fine Arts Department.

Most importantly, the relocation of the college in 1931 generated a sense of beginning again, and the new campus gave Little Rock Junior College an identity the institution had lacked when classes met in the high school building.

Part of the spirit of starting over also resulted from a change in the administration of the college. Throughout the school's 30-year existence, LRJC had been unique in its functioning as a privately financed school under public control. Tax support for the institution was prohibited by state law, yet the publicly elected Little Rock School Board continued to be the school's governing body, and a public school superintendent and principal served as president and dean respectively. After the move Superintendent Hall stepped down and Larson (continuing to serve as principal of Little Rock Senior High School) became the new president of Little Rock Junior College. The school board designated E.Q. Brothers as the new dean.

A native of Kansas, Brothers had worked in the educational hierarchy of his native state before being named dean. Because of the demands on Larson's time as principal of the high school, Brothers in effect served as Little Rock Junior College's chief executive officer, overseeing the daily operation of the school throughout the 1930s and early 1940s. He worked on curriculum development and expansion of the physical plant and in many instances personally selected new faculty members.[8] Brothers actively promoted the junior college movement; in 1934 the membership of the American Association of Junior Colleges chose him as their national president, marking the first time the organization had picked an individual to lead the group who did not also hold a position as a junior college president.[9]

While not particularly dynamic, Brothers worked well with the college faculty and oversaw the day-to-day functioning of the school for over 20 years.

J.H. Atkinson, noted Arkansas historian and instructor at LRJC from 1927 to 1957. (1959 **Trojan)**

One instructor later remembered that Brothers "was not a man who pushed himself. He was not a great one to go out and speak to civic clubs and wave the flag for the J.C. But I think the community leaders had great respect for him."[10] Larson also thought Brothers was a valuable asset to the college. In the early 1930s, when many salaries had to be cut because of the Depression, Larson fought with the school board to get a raise for the new dean.[11]

One of Brothers's primary responsibilities involved teacher recruitment, and between 1931 and 1935 his efforts produced a solid junior college teaching staff that became the nucleus of the school's faculty for the next two decades. Teaching in a two-year college resembled instruction at the secondary level, and instructors considered themselves primarily classroom teachers rather than research-oriented scholars. The Jaycee staff worked hard in performing their classroom duties, and in an annual report from the era President Larson succinctly described his faculty as "(1) Well trained (2) Devoted (3) Underpaid."[12]

Some Jaycee teachers did have scholarly interests outside their classrooms. For example, J.H. Atkinson later became known as "Mr. Arkansas history" for his endeavors in the field of local history.[13] A native of Columbia County, Atkinson was a graduate of the University of Arkansas and held a master's degree from the University of Chicago. He had taught in a series of rural Arkansas schools before coming to Little Rock Senior High School in 1916. After a brief tenure as a school superintendent at Wilmot between 1919 and 1923, Atkinson returned as the head of the high

school history department at Little Rock between 1923 and 1927. In 1927 he became chairman of the Department of History and Economics at Little Rock Junior College, a position he held until his retirement in 1957. As part of his interest in the state's past, Atkinson founded the Pulaski County Historical Society, served as president of the Arkansas Historical Association, produced dozens of articles on the state's history, and edited the *Arkansas Historical Quarterly* between 1941 and 1963. One colleague later referred to him as "the most significant personality in the field of Arkansas history for the past thirty years,"[14] and generations of Jaycee students found Atkinson to be a stimulating classroom teacher and informal counselor. "I'm really interested in trying to help students with their problems," he once told an interviewer. "I don't mean math or English problems. The real problem for a great many college students is to adjust themselves to living with their fellows."[15]

Pauline Hoeltzel was another original faculty member who remained at Little Rock Junior College for over 20 years and earned a reputation as an excellent classroom teacher. An English instructor, Hoeltzel served for several years as faculty advisor to the yearbook and newspaper, coordinator of alumni activities, and chairman of the Humanities Division. In 1949 voters in an informal poll selected her Little Rock's "Woman of the Year." In addition, Arkansas governor Sid McMath appointed her to the Board of Trustees of the University of Arkansas, making her the first woman to receive that honor.[16]

Hoeltzel's colleagues in the English department included Gladys Kunz

*Pauline Hoeltzel, chairman of the Humanities Division and instructor in English and German at LRJC from 1927 to 1964. (1964 **Trojan,** 48)*

Brown and Dorothy Yarnell, who both taught for many years at LRJC and actively participated in numerous student and faculty activities outside their classroom duties. Blanche Martin served as the college's first Dean of Women in the early 1930s after heading the mathematics department at Little Rock Senior High School for twelve years. In 1932 Mrs. Dell Park McDermott joined the faculty as an instructor in the speech and drama department and over the course of her seventeen years at the school, according to another instructor, "made her department one of the most outstanding ones in the state."[17]

The early teaching staff at LRJC also included Madame Florence Hemans, a French and Spanish instructor who taught at the college for fifteen years and developed a reputation for being extremely dramatic in her class presentations; Rabbi Ira E. Sanders, who taught sociology for several years before becoming one of Little Rock's most respected clergymen; and M.F. Moose, an able scholar who taught both physics and chemistry. John Gould Fletcher, a Little Rock native and a prominent poet of the Imagist school, credited the above-mentioned Blanche Martin with encouraging his writing career when he studied under her in high school. In the mid-1930s he taught a class in Romantic English literature at Jaycee, and a few years later he received the Pulitzer Prize for poetry.

While the addition of new faculty members enhanced the feeling of starting over at the campus at Thirteenth and State, that spirit increased with changes in the college's curriculum. Faced with growing problems generated by the nationwide depression, school officials altered the LRJC program to meet students' changing needs — that is, by adding more vocationally oriented courses to the general curriculum, while not abandoning the institution's liberal arts core. In January 1932 Jaycee authorities initiated a program in secretarial training to "develop high-class secretaries, clerks, and office help."[18] The following fall the school added courses in surveying and pattern-making, along with brief non-credit courses in areas like health, recreation, and parent education.

As the school began offering more courses, the faculty worked to restrict the number of hours a student might carry in a single semester. By 1934 the instructional staff defined a normal workload as fifteen to sixteen semester-hours in one term and prohibited anyone from carrying more than eighteen hours without the consent of the dean of the college.[19] In addition, rules pertaining to class attendance allowed no unexcused absences, and school policy dictated that two tardies constituted one absence.[20] To raise scholastic standards, starting in 1934, school officials demanded that students have a minimum of 60 grade points in order to graduate. A grade of A in a course earned three grade points, a B earned two grade points, and a C merited only one. A student who passed 60 credit hours without the required grade points had to carry additional hours until he or she reached the required 60 grade points.[21]

To improve the academic standing of the institution further, school officials upgraded the college library when LRJC moved to the new campus in 1931. By closing the second-floor hall, the administration created space for the library,

The 1933 Little Rock Junior College Band. (1933 **Trojan)**

and the Donaghey Foundation provided funding for new chairs and tables. Jaycee's library contained approximately 5,283 volumes, many of which had been contributed by members of the faculty. Almost 90 percent of the books dealt with literature, history, biography, and the social sciences, leaving a notable gap in the physical sciences, fine arts, and vocational areas of the curriculum.[22] In 1933, however, the administration appointed the first faculty library committee and the members labored for several years to correct imbalances in the library holdings.

Along with the volumes provided by the library, students could purchase books and other materials at the Jaycee bookstore. Organized in 1927 when local book dealers refused to handle college books, the junior college outlet operated in conjunction with the high school bookstore. After the move to Thirteenth and State, President Larson established a separate bookstore in the west end of the main corridor under the direction of a student manager who received half of his tuition and fees for supervising the operation. Profits from the store went to the band, the football team, or some other needy student group.[23]

In the early 1930s nearly every student organization as well as individual students needed money, for LRJC, like virtually all American institutions, suffered the effects of the Depression. The collapse of the economy hit students particularly hard, forcing many promising undergraduates to abandon or postpone their educational plans. Some institutions of higher education had to curtail their programs, dismiss faculty, and struggle for several years to remain open. In Little Rock a drought in the

summer of 1930 aggravated the local business failures, mortgage foreclosures, bank closings, and chronic unemployment that threatened citizens' security.

Nevertheless, the newly relocated junior college weathered the initial years of the Depression surprisingly well. Although at first faculty members feared they might not get paid on a regular basis because of the school's financial difficulties, the teaching staff never missed a paycheck throughout the decade. In some ways the Depression actually strengthened the college. One faculty member later recalled that "young people who just couldn't go away to the University or State Teachers ... came to the J.C. And in those years we had a suprising number of sons and daughters of very well-known Little Rock families."[24] Still, the overall enrollment of the college suffered a slight decline. During the 1930-31 school year, Little Rock Junior College had 441 students, but by January 1934 the student body had dropped to 350.[25]

Along with dwindling numbers of students, school officials faced the problem of many undergraduates' inability to pay their tuition. Because Jaycee depended almost entirely on tuition for revenue this situation posed a serious difficulty. Unfortunately, the cost of attending LRJC rivaled the expense of other institutions in the state. A 1935 survey revealed that the average tuition and fees of five denominational colleges in Arkansas equaled $146 while at LRJC tuition and fees for a standard course load equaled $147.50.[26]

To help students pay for their education during the Depression, junior college officials established a lenient credit policy. The College Chatter also inaugu-

*Elmer C. Stahlkopf, economics and political science instructor at Jaycee for 36 years. (1966 **Trojan,** 54)*

rated a scholarship loan fund, and in 1933 the school launched a program to admit academically talented students who lacked one year of completing high school and might want to shorten the time they would have to spend in school. LRJC students held a wide variety of part-time jobs, working as undertakers, playground supervisors, theater ushers, cashiers, and bakers. Others delivered the local newspapers, drove buses, or worked in the Chatter Grill. Beginning in 1933, managers of the Donaghey Building established a new policy that if any maintenance or other job became vacant in the building, only LRJC students would be considered to fill the post.[27] In addition to these positions, around 60 Jaycee students found employment through the National Youth Administration, one of President Franklin D. Roosevelt's New Deal programs to combat the Depression. Paid 25 cents an hour and tuition allotments, the NYA workers performed a variety of tasks for the local Boys' Club, YMCA, YWCA, and other educational and civic organizations.[28]

These students who worked at part-time jobs established a tradition that remained a characteristic of the institution. Even after Jaycee became Little Rock University and later the University of Arkansas at Little Rock, the college maintained a high percentage of students who worked while attending classes. While undoubtedly this practice hurt the academic performance of some young people by limiting their study time, the presence of so many undergraduates working their way through school often contributed to an atmosphere of seriousness and purpose on the campus.

Even with a large number of working students, college life at Jaycee continued as usual during the early years of the Depression with even a heightened sense of community among students and faculty. In a later interview, one teacher remembered the era as a time filled with picnics and dances attended by both undergraduates and instructors. "The faculty knew each other and the students all knew each other well," she said. "There was a very close relationship between faculty and students."[29] Another instructor remembered dances held at the Shrine Country Club and recalled "the stroll over the grounds in the late afternoon, the formal dinner and dance ... events never to be forgotten."[30] Students and teachers often shared light moments even in the midst of the economic difficulties of the era. On one occasion Elmer Stahlkopf, an instructor who taught at the college for many years, asked students on an examination in his "Money and Banking" class to explain what caused economic depressions. One student responded, "God only knows, I don't." Stahlkopf then wrote on the paper, "God gets a hundred, you get nothing."[31]

Student organizations also fostered a sense of comaraderie among the young men and women who attended Little Rock Junior College. One such group was the International Relations Club, organized in November 1931 under the sponsorship of J.H. Atkinson, and affiliated with a national organization designed to promote world peace under the auspices of the Carnegie Foundation. The club quickly became prominent on campus. In 1934 it hosted the Southwest Conference of International Relations Clubs. Over 100 delegates from 22 colleges in four states attended the meeting at the Albert Pike Hotel, and according to Atkinson the conference "gave the college a big boost both in the eyes of the students and in the eyes of the public."[32]

Atkinson also sponsored the Trojan Forum, the school's debate society. In 1932 the debaters affiliated with Phi Rho Pi, the national junior college forensic society, and throughout the decade participated in debating tournaments and made speeches to civic and business organizations on behalf of the Community Chest and other charitable agencies.[33]

In 1931, a year before LRJC formed a formal speech department, students presented three plays. *H.M.S. Pinafore,* under the direction of chemistry instructor Kenneth Bird, drew an audience of over 1000 people for a single performance at the high school auditorium and featured a large chorus, including William (Casey) Laman, a future mayor of North Little Rock.[34] In 1932, interested students organized Song and Satire, a musical and artistic group supplementary to the Jaycee Masquers, the dramatic club organized in 1929.

The early 1930s also witnessed the rise of the *College Chatter* to the forefront of collegiate newspapers in the state. In 1932 the *Chatter* won a trophy as the state's best all-around college paper at a collegiate journalism meeting in Clarksville, an honor it went on to earn for seven consecutive years.[35] Over the course of the decade, the paper ran an annual literary edition providing students with a forum for their poems, essays, and stories, and the *Chatter* also led campus reform efforts to improve parking, to beautify the campus, and to

raise academic standards.

Along with service and academic associations, Little Rock Junior College had a limited number of social organizations in the first few years at the Thirteenth and State campus. Organized in the fall of 1927, Phi Alpha Beta became the first men's social fraternity at LRJC, while in 1932 a women's group called the Battlecriers, which began as a booster organization for Trojan athletics, evolved into Jaycee's first sorority. Also in 1932 a second fraternity, Delta Kappa, appeared at the college and soon initiated a spirited rivalry with the older Phi Alpha Beta.

For several years after the relocation, football remained an important focus of campus activity. In the fall of 1931 the Trojan team earned the school's first gridiron victory with a 13-12 win over El Dorado Junior College at El Dorado. A few weeks later, on November 20, 1931, Jaycee held the school's first annual Homecoming celebration, which featured a special assembly, a parade through downtown Little Rock, a football game (which the Trojans lost to Fort Smith Junior College 6-0), and a dance.[36] Although football games provided a social outlet for the students, the LRJC teams won few games in the early 1930s; one dismal afternoon the Trojans fell to Texarkana Junior College by a score of 86-0.[37] In 1935 school officials dropped football at the college.

Student life at Jaycee during these years also included biweekly assemblies, featuring programs arranged by a joint student-faculty committee and chapel services conducted by local ministers once or twice each month. A reorganized LRJC government included a student-executive council with representatives from each major campus organization. Typically, many students voiced criticism of the student government's lack of achievement, and a 1932 *Chatter* editorial writer voiced a universal undergraduate complaint when he wrote, "We want to know if the Student Council is just a figurehead or if they are ever going to … start accomplishing things."[38]

If the Student Council failed to meet the writer's expectations, other campus associations achieved considerable success in establishing events and activities that became traditional at LRJC for the next quarter-century. In 1935 a joint student-faculty committee selected a composition by Blanche Markham from entries in a contest sponsored by the *Trojan* to be Jaycee's official school song:

Hail LRJC, Hail to thy name!
We'll wave thy colors, Long sing
    thy fame!
Maroon and White forever! Loyal
    we'll be;
Our Alma Mater, LRJC![39]

Three events organized in the early 1930s became annual activities integral to campus life. On November 11, 1931, Jaycee sponsored Stunt Night at the high school auditorium, where various clubs and societies presented ten-minute skits to raise money for the student loan fund. Held every year thereafter, Stunt Night grew in scope and became so successful that as late as the 1950s one student writer commented that with its carnival atmosphere, door prizes, and general spirit of fun, "Stunt Night has been the one event of the school year that all students look forward to."[40]

Self-Expression Week also became a significant part of the school calendar.

Originally called Speech-Journalism Week because the activites showcased original one-act plays, oratorical contests, and writing competitions, the event became Self-Expression Week in 1934, when faculty sponsors decided to include performances by students in the music department. The scope expanded to include shorthand and typing contests and stage and costume design competitions. In 1939 Mrs. W.F. Hall, an instructor and one of the originators of Self-Expression Week, defined the scope of the event: "the purpose of the week's activities is to have a … student enterprise whereby the young people may have the opportunity to display their individual talents and accomplishments in free competition with their classmates."[41]

Rivaling Stunt Night and Self-Expression Week in terms of popularity, Donaghey Week was a series of activities held each spring to recognize the school's chief benefactor. Organized in 1932 around the theme "Honor to Whom Honor Is Due," the annual Donaghey Week celebration became "a time of banquets, assemblies, radio programs, and parades of lively students, full of fervor and school spirit."[42] For many years Governor and Mrs. Donaghey attended the annual banquet. Several years after the governor's death in 1937, Mrs. Donaghey told an interviewer that "Donaghey Week is the biggest week of my life. I look forward to it all year."[43]

The inauguration of campus traditions like these generated a spirit of optimism at LRJC in the early 1930s. Despite the haunting specter of the Depression, students and faculty expressed confidence that their fledgling institution would grow and prosper. As early as

1929 one student editor wrote that "already the school is well on the way toward being the greatest junior college in the South,"[44] and three years later another writer observed that LRJC "is at last taking its place among the leading educational institutions of the state."[45]

Atkinson credited the achievements of the college to John Larson's leadership.[46] Indeed, within a few years of the school's founding, Larson's positive assessment of LRJC's future led to support for expansion of the school. As early as 1932, only five years after the creation of the tiny two-year institution that held classes in the local high school, campus leaders referred to the "dream of a four-year municipal university … [to be established] maybe three years from now, maybe five years from now." Even George Donaghey commented in 1932 that "we can have a four-year university within a year's time…."[47]

That same year an LRJC student named Maurice Spitzberg succinctly stated the basic argument that would be used for over 20 years by advocates of extending the junior college program. "We ought to have a municipal university because we are the largest and most important city in Arkansas," Spitzberg said. "No other city compares with Little Rock in the facilities offered to such an institution. Various kinds of courses and jobs for the students who wish to work their way through college are among the advantages offered by Little Rock, and for the most part by Little Rock alone."[48]

Despite this early optimism, Little Rock Junior College continued as a two-year-institution for a quarter-century. While the dream of a four-year college remained a long-range goal of those in-dividuals connected with the school, their efforts focused primarily on providing the best possible education to the students of the capital city through a junior college structure. In maintaining that orientation, the faculty and administration of LRJC weathered the remainder of the Depression and guided the school through the difficult years of World War II. Their work over the decade from 1935 to 1945 consequently provided not only the basis for what many would later regard as the junior college's "golden age" in the late 1940s, but also kept alive the hope of someday building a municipal university on that foundation.

C H A P T E R   F O U R

The Peanut Butter College

*T*hroughout the 1930s, the junior college movement gained momentum nationwide. An increasing number of educational leaders acknowledged that the thirteenth and fourteenth years of the educational system had become as important as high school training had been a few decades earlier, and more collegiate educators recognized the value of two-year institutions. In 1941 the Dean of Harvard College announced that "because of the growth and development of junior colleges in recent years, the committee on admissions ... have changed their rules to allow J.C. students to transfer."[1] In Little Rock, after the movement to convert LRJC to a municipal university declined because of financial considerations, school authorities concentrated on improving the college's overall program and making the institution a quality junior college.

Unfortunately, these efforts often went unnoticed in the Little Rock community. In 1938 Dorothy Yarnell conducted a survey of local newspapers and found that Hendrix College in Conway and Arkansas Polytechnical College in Russellville received the most coverage of all institutions of higher education in Arkansas, while Little Rock Junior College received the least. Yarnell's study indicated that almost all stories about

LRJC "were buried in the Little Rock public school news,"[2] leaving the people of central Arkansas largely unaware of the development of one of the few successful colleges in the city. This lack of publicity proved to be especially detrimental since the years between 1935 and 1940 marked a period of rapid growth and maturity at Little Rock Junior College.

A $6000 grant to the college from the Carnegie Corporation in the fall of 1937 provided one of the first indications that LRJC had achieved a measure of recognition among the nation's junior colleges.[3] Designed to upgrade the library, the grant was not paid in money but in books selected by the college and purchased by the corporation. Little Rock Junior College was one of only ten schools selected to receive the maximum award of $6000, which the Carnegie Foundation paid in annual installments of $2000 for three years. Since at the time of the award the library was functioning on only about $550 a year, the Carnegie gift was a windfall that greatly enhanced the school's library facilities. By the end of 1938 LRJC library holdings had increased to over 13,000 volumes.[4]

The college library also benefited from the able administration of Vera E. Hardcastle, who became librarian in the fall of 1937. Under Hardcastle's direction the library grew by over 900 feet of shelving space, and staff members recatalogued all of the volumes in the collection, using printed cards provided by the Library of Congress. Hardcastle also inaugurated a "Browsing Nook" to encourage students to read outside their class assignments in an area that featured a bowl of fresh marigolds, comfortable chairs, and almost 500 titles of entertaining fiction and non-fiction books.[5]

In addition to the library grant, the Carnegie Corporation awarded a $1500 music set to LRJC in 1938. Obtained through the joint efforts of Dean Brothers and members of the school's music department, the equipment included a phonograph and a collection of 620 phonograph records designed for the "cultural development of undergraduates."[6]

Between 1939 and 1944 the institution was also one of 22 colleges to share in a cooperative study in general education. A committee of the American Council of Education and the General Education Board, searching for colleges "which had already proved themselves open-minded and interested in progressive ideas," selected only two colleges in Arkansas to participate — Little Rock Junior College and Hendrix College in Conway.[7]

The general education movement after World War I stemmed from a reaction among American educators to what they thought were overly materialistic and scientific trends in education. They blamed the elective system of American colleges and universities for producing a generation of specialists who lacked a broad appreciation of the humanizing aspects of life.[8] These reformers argued that a society whose members lacked a body of common experience and knowledge "degenerated into fragmented individuals without a fundamental culture."[9] The solution they recommended lay in the concept of general education — a new emphasis on a well-rounded education stressing Western values, ideas, and attitudes at the expense of more specialized and technical training. The general education movement gained widespread notoriety for a few years, but the demands of World War II and the Cold War that followed dictated a return to specialized training, and general education lost popularity in the democratized world of postwar higher education.

As part of the experimental study in the late 1930s, however, Little Rock Junior College offered a series of survey courses in the arts and sciences aimed at providing students with an introduction to "all fields of human knowledge rather than specialized information."[10] Beginning with a social science survey course in 1939 and later expanding to include similar six-hour courses in humanities, physical science, and the arts, LRJC's experiment proved only moderately successful. While George A. Barton of the Department of Education at the University of Chicago found Jaycee's survey course in art to be "one of the most carefully planned courses that I have encountered,"[11] many LRJC instructors and undergraduates felt the physical science survey course lacked focus and failed to achieve the aims of the program.[12] Like many other institutions, Little Rock Junior College felt growing pressures for a more vocationally oriented curriculum, and abandoned a formal program of general education during World War II.

Still, the goals of the reform movement remained a vital part of the school's educational philosophy. In 1949, for example, a public relations brochure published by Jaycee stated, "[T]he curriculum of LRJC has as its foundation a program of general education. In this program the student is made aware of the artistic, intellectual, and spiritual life of the past ...."[13]

As the college strove to gain academic maturity in the 1930s, school officials also promoted the physical growth of the institution. In the latter part of the decade the LRJC campus expanded to include an auditorium-gymnasium, a chemistry laboratory, and five temporary classroom buildings salvaged from U.S. army surplus. Built partly from material acquired when Little Rock public school authorities tore down the grandstand at Kavanaugh Field, the auditorium-gymnasium was constructed with the aid of workers furnished by the New Deal's Works Progress Administration and was partly financed with a public fund-raising campaign[14] and a donation from the Donaghey Foundation. Students first used the new structure in November 1937 by throwing a "Thug Party," where revellers arrived dressed as gangsters, burglars, and other unlawful citizens.[15]

WPA-financed workers also built a small cafeteria annex, constructed a recreation room for women students in the east basement, and paved Thirteenth Street in front of the campus with material provided by the college and other property owners on the street. Using plans designed by Dean Brothers, chemistry department chairman M.F. Moose, and engineering department chairman

Guy Irby, WPA employees also built a chemistry laboratory on the northwest corner of the campus.[16] These additions proved adequate for the college's needs until a wave of returning World War II veterans forced school officials to consider a second relocation of the entire plant.

The physical and other improvements at Jaycee in the 1930s required additional financial support, which President Larson and the rest of the administration worked hard and creatively to provide. Because many students had difficulty paying their school expenses, Jaycee authorities initiated a system that both aided needy undergraduates and spurred tuition collection. In the fall of 1939 school officials circulated a mimeographed sheet announcing that "if students will pay their tuition notes on the dates they are due, they will be given a five percent discount on that part of the tuition."[17]

LRJC officials also utilized an annual "Tag Day" to increase revenues for the college. On a specified day in spring, members of the Little Rock Parent-Teacher Association collected money from citizens on the streets of downtown Little Rock. In return for each gift, the PTA volunteers pinned a tag on the contributor, showing that the person had supported the drive. In addition to the downtown solicitation on Tag Day, school officials sought funds through a mail campaign and from boxes placed in each of the city's public schools. In 1940 over 100 women assisted in the Tag Day efforts and raised $489 for a Jaycee scholarship fund.[18]

Scholarships provided important subsidies for students attending Little Rock Junior College during the Depression. In

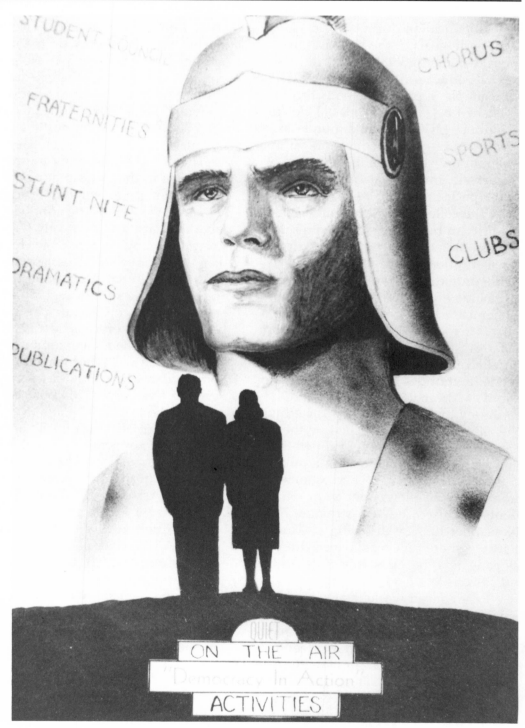

*The **Trojan,** 1940 style.*

the mid-1930s almost one-third of the student body received some kind of scholarship aid. Funds for these awards came from the Little Rock Senior High School Parent-Teacher Association, the Donaghey Foundation, the Abigail Robinson Scholarship Fund, Lamar Porter, and the LRJC Alumni Association. In addition, all honor graduates and valedictorians of high schools in the state automatically received a scholarship to attend Jaycee.

Along with money from gifts and tuition, Little Rock Junior College relied on funds from the Donaghey Foundation. In October 1937 Governor Donaghey again made a significant gift to the school by donating an additional $100,000 in downtown real estate to the Jaycee endowment. The grant included the southwest corner of Seventh and Main Streets, the site of the Majestic Theater, and a lot at 117 Main Street.

Two months after making the gift to the college, in December 1937, George Donaghey died. According to the campus newspaper, upon hearing of the ex-governor's death the students and faculty of LRJC "stood grief-stricken and inarticulate,"[19] and a few days later a large delegation from the college community attended the funeral of the school's leading benefactor.

Immediately following Donaghey's death, political figures and educators publicly praised his generous support of higher education, and several community leaders suggested changing the name of Little Rock Junior College to Donaghey College. Little Rock mayor R.E. Overman, County Judge J.G. Burlingame, and Mrs. Gladys Richards, president of the Business and Professional Women's Club, all actively sup-

ported the new name. Dean Brothers of the college concurred: "I have long been waiting for the time that the name might be changed to Donaghey College."[20]

Those who wanted to remember the governor by naming the college in his honor were disappointed when members of the Little Rock School Board refused to give the school a new designation. The hope that someday the college would bear the name of its most generous supporter lingered until the mid-1950s when officials decided to rename the school "Little Rock University" — a move that even then generated opposition from long-time supporters of "Donaghey College."

Although the college never bore his name, Donaghey's generosity provided the school with a financial foundation that insured its survival. Yet by the early 1940s school officials recognized that income from gifts, tuition, and the Donaghey Foundation might prove inadequate to meet the educational needs of the next generation of LRJC students, and consequently in 1942 they joined other interested parties in an effort to remove the state's legal prohibition against a local tax to support junior colleges. Arkansas legislators had resisted the measure since the 1920s because they feared a proliferation of tiny junior colleges that would use money needed for primary and secondary education.

In 1939 a bill to allow such a tax passed the Arkansas Senate, but was narrowly defeated by members of the House of Representatives at the close of the legislative session. Three years later, in November 1942, a similar measure appeared on the ballot as a proposed amendment to the state constitution.

Since the junior college tax had the support of newspapers and educational and civic leaders throughout the state, the Jaycee community felt confident the school would soon have public support. However, the state's voters defeated Amendment 32. Shocked officials at LRJC attributed the defeat to ignorance of the nature of the amendment, reluctance to raise taxes, and voter apathy[21] and resigned themselves to educating the city's young people with funds available from tuition, gifts, and Donaghey Foundation revenue.

The responsibility for that educational process fell largely on the LRJC faculty, who continued to regard themselves as classroom instructors rather than research-oriented scholars. To that end they maintained active memberships in the Arkansas Education Association, a statewide professional organization whose membership came primarily from public school teachers and administrators.[22]

On the Jaycee campus most full-time instructors taught fifteen semester-hours of classes each term, sponsored student clubs, and served on a variety of committees covering areas like entertainment, employment, publicity, class schedules, the academic calendar, recreation, "sunshine," and social events. Dean Brothers assigned faculty members to committees at the beginning of the school year and most teachers served on at least two. Only in 1941 did the Jaycee instructors join the retirement plan offered by the prestigious Teachers Annuity and Insurance Association of America. Despite low salaries the teaching staff at Little Rock Junior College during the latter years of the Depression did its job with the same sense of duty

and devotion to education that characterized so many public school teachers of the era.

Student life at Little Rock Junior College in the 1930s reflected the growth of the institution as a whole. Young people who attended the school during that era engaged in numerous activities that ranged from serious social and economic programs to some endeavors that bordered on being ridiculous and even dangerous.

Some of the most publicized events in the life of the college during those years involved the rise and fall and then the resurrection of men's social fraternities. Before 1935 two fraternities, Phi Alpha Beta and Delta Kappa, had existed without official recognition by the college administration. However, in 1935 the members of Delta Kappa committed an act so reprehensible that the Little Rock School Board banned all fraternities and sororities from the campus for over two years.

That year the DKs, as part of their initiation ritual, took six initiates to a deserted rock quarry and painted their faces with a solution of silver nitrate. The chemical caused the boys' heads and faces to swell to almost twice their normal size, and, unable to get help, the young men spent several hours in great pain until they could make their way to the city hospital. Doctors at first believed the boys' faces would be permanently disfigured but through the efforts of a dermatologist the worst ravages of the accident disappeared after about six months.[23]

The editor of the *College Chatter* wrote that the incident had "left a permanent mark on the college" and argued that the injuries could have been avoided if the college had officially recognized the fraternity and supervised the group's activities.[24] The Little Rock School Board took a different approach. For several years board members had been uncomfortable with social clubs at Little Rock Senior High School because the groups' discriminatory nature demoralized students who failed to gain membership. Using the events surrounding the Delta Kappa initiation tragedy as a catalyst, on May 26, 1935, the board passed a resolution "abolishing all secret fraternities, sororities, and clubs in all schools under jurisdiction of the Little Rock School Board, including Little Rock Junior College."[25]

On the Jaycee campus, students and faculty members resented the board's ruling, arguing that undergraduates should not be governed by the same rules as local grammar school pupils. The entire incident highlighted the identity crisis that had plagued the junior college since the its founding eight years earlier. The college wanted to be seen as a separate facility for higher education, while in reality it functioned as an extension of the local public school system.

In April 1936 a delegation of junior college students, led by student body president Joe W. Sitlington, petitioned the school board for permission to operate social fraternities again on the campus. The representatives presented a document signed by thirteen of the sixteen instructors at the college stating that teachers did not oppose junior college fraternities if faculty members supervised the groups. Despite this display of faculty support, the board denied the students' request.[26]

That year the Little Rock School Board established a special committee to oversee the activities of the junior college. This recognition that the affairs of LRJC needed to be treated separately from those of the city's elementary schools, junior highs, and high schools helped to clarify the identity of the school. In the fall of 1937 LRJC students presented a petition signed by almost 80 percent of their parents urging the Little Rock School Board's approval of fraternities and sororities, and upon the recommendation of the junior college committee, the board lifted the ban. Hearing of the board's decision, one student commented, "[I]t is not so much a victory for the fraternity as it is for the college," and the editor of the campus paper wrote that "the school board gave dignity to Jaycee as a college ... for the first time [the board] made public acknowledgment that LRJC is a college and should be treated as a college ...."[27]

Almost immediately, Phi Alpha Beta became the first social fraternity recognized by LRJC authorities. A faculty-student committee established a set of rules to regulate the club, including provisions for a faculty advisor and a stipulation that fraternity members had to maintain a C average in their academic work. In February 1938 Delta Kappa gained acceptance by the administration under the same rules, and for many years the two men's organizations maintained an intense rivalry that affected not only the recruitment of members and intramural athletics, but also other campus activities such as student elections.[28] For female students, the Battlecriers began functioning as a social sorority rather than a booster club, and the Tri Phi sorority gained recognition in the spring of 1938.[29]

The granting of spring holidays also showed an acknowledgment that the junior college deserved to be treated differently from other city schools. For several years LRJC students had actively supported the idea of a spring vacation like that of other colleges, but the faculty had opposed the idea. In late 1936 the situation changed when Dorothy Yarnell addressed a faculty meeting and spoke in favor of the holidays. With her support, a group of students led by Joe Truemper and Charles Carpenter applied to the school board for a Jaycee spring vacation.[30] On January 20, 1937, the board voted to grant Easter holidays to the junior college, and a year later spring vacation became a permanent part of the college calendar. Little Rock Junior College was finally being accepted as a collegiate institution distinct from the city's high school program.

During this era, the college's athletic program also underwent fundamental changes. From the school's inception in 1927 and continuing through the Little Rock University and University of Arkansas years, school officials struggled to find a proper role for varsity athletics at the college. At times the leadership of the institution deemed a competitive intercollegiate sports program to be essential for recruiting alumni support, raising student morale, and improving the school's image in the community and the state. At other times the administration found such a program an excessively expensive and unnecessary part of the school's extracurricular activities and restricted the role of athletics on the campus to intramural competition.

In the late summer of 1935 the school board abolished football and placed

a new stress on intramurals — fencing, swimming, tennis, basketball, boxing, and rifle shooting. Although the varsity basketball team (which earlier played all home games at the Little Rock Boys' Club) inaugurated the school's new gymnasium in the winter of 1938 with a narrow victory over Magnolia A&M,[31] a year later the administration abolished Trojan basketball at LRJC. Citing financial difficulties and lack of skilled players as reasons for the abandonment of football and basketball, the college's leadership continued to promote the institution's intramural program.

During the years of deemphasis of varsity sports, Little Rock Junior College did experience some athletic successes: a greater percentage of students took an active role in intramural competitions, and an LRJC fencing team coached by John Fuhrhop of the local YMCA placed third in the Southwest Fencing Tournament in Dallas, in 1937. On the other hand, students expressed disappointment at the lack of collegiate spirit usually generated by interscholastic competition, and many traditional campus activities were modified in ways that proved unpopular with the student body. School officials replaced the annual Homecoming Day, which had traditionally featured a football game with an assembly program, a lawn luncheon, and a dance at the Women's City Club for Alumni Day, and once-popular booster organizations like the Sports Club had to disband.

Student morale in the late thirties also declined at LRJC as students attempted to lessen faculty restrictions on their behavior. The Grill, traditionally the most popular on-campus gathering place for students, became almost deserted by the spring of 1939 because of administration prohibitions against a nickelodean, dancing, and bridge playing, which the faculty felt encouraged gambling.[32] That same year instructors further alienated some students by pressuring them to purchase tickets to the annual Donaghey Day luncheon. With ticket sales lagging, Dean Brothers had told the teachers at a faculty meeting to "contact [your] advisees and try to sell them tickets."[33]

Certainly not all campus activities had a demoralizing effect on the students, and social life at Jaycee generally went on as usual. Each year the social calendar featured one or two faculty-student parties that sometimes included activities that would impress a later generation of college students as being somewhat childish. For example, one such function in the early 1940s began with a musical game called "Pickin' Up Paw Paws," in which each contestant gathered up a chair, an umbrella, a bucket, and a whistle and then ran to a designated area and unfolded the chair, raised the umbrella, ate a cracker, and blew the whistle.[34] A few years earlier Jaycee students also joined the nationwide craze of "knock-knock" jokes. Originally called "Punology" from a song by Vincent Lopez, knock-knock jokes were enormously popular on the nation's college campuses in the fall of 1936.[35]

Movies and popular music also provided Jaycee students with a link with their counterparts on other campuses. A 1938 poll indicated LRJC students favored the big band sounds of Tommy Dorsey and Benny Goodman and movies featuring Frederick March and Claudette Colbert.[36] Locally, the student body participated in annual events like the Farmers' Ball at the Women's City

Club and the campus YMCA's minstrel show at the Boys' Club along with weekly tea dances in the new gymnasium.[37] Stunt Night continued to grow in popularity. In 1943 it included a well-received faculty skit under the direction of Pauline Hoeltzel; the event raised money for the Student Loan Fund and always received generous support from local businesses.

Student activities of the era were by no means limited to social events. Many young people who attended the junior college in the years before World War II devoted considerable energy to academic and vocational interests. Their successes helped combat the popular image that junior college students tended to be less intelligent and self-motivated than those who attended traditional four-year institutions. This unflattering portrait had plagued the junior college movement from the beginning and received support from well-known educators like James Bryant Conant, who regarded two-year colleges primarily as institutions "for students who did not have sufficient ability to 'make the grade' at regular four year colleges."[38] Even Dean Brothers admitted in the early 1940s that "there has been somewhat of a let-down in fundamentals, such as reading and arithmetic."[39]

Despite these comments and the popular image of the inferiority of junior college students, numerous studies by professional educators indicated a wide range of abilities among students who attended two-year colleges.[40] One nationwide survey conducted in the 1940s showed that while the average achievement scores for junior college freshmen were several points below those of freshmen attending traditional

Robert Gannaway and Amanda Duna-
way, the popularly elected King and Queen
of the campus in 1938.

liberal arts colleges, they were much higher than those of first-year students at four-year teachers' colleges. The same study also revealed that undergraduates who transferred from junior colleges to senior institutions generally fared well academically.[41]

The Little Rock Junior College student body in the 1930s and early 1940s included a group of achievers who were highly motivated and capable. In 1937 LRJC's Alpha Alpha chapter of Phi Theta Kappa, the junior college scholastic fraternity, hosted the organization's national convention. Geneva Perry, the local president, presided over the general sessions at West Side Junior High School at Fourteenth and Marshall Streets. During World War II, when no conventions could be held, Phi Theta Kappa's national executive committee met twice in Little Rock, and the Alpha Alpha chapter contributed several officers: Thomas Rutledge served as national treasurer in 1940-41, Betty Blaylock as president in 1944-45, and Sue Patillo as president in 1945-46. As late as 1956, Jaycee students remained active in the honorary group, promoting the successful candidacy of Gene McNabb as second vice-president of the organization. Locally, Phi Theta Kappa sponsored an annual Founders' Day Banquet and an Honors Night, held each year during commencement week to present various academic and other awards to Jaycee students.[42]

In 1936 Little Rock Junior College students had another opportunity to exhibit responsibility when the *College Chatter* suddenly had to depend entirely on advertising to pay for the printing of the paper. The *Chatter* of the era ran news stories, gossip columns, sports reports, and faculty notes and provided an important bond among students. Pauline Hoeltzel, faculty sponsor of the paper in the thirties, later compared the role of the paper before World War II with its function after the school reached university status. "Everybody was more interested in little things then they are now," she said. "Nobody cares now whether Susie Smith has a party or not because they probably don't know Susie Smith."[43] Prior to 1936 the Jaycee newspaper had been printed as a project of the Little Rock Senior High School printing class, but when school officials made the high school paper a weekly, the *Chatter* staff had to use a commercial printer.[44] The junior college students consequently accelerated their efforts to sell advertising to local businesses. As a result the *Chatter* continued to publish campus news, and the college and the community developed an important link that lasted for several years.

Another important connection between Jaycee and the citizens of Little Rock came from the activities of the Trojan Theater Guild. The Guild, started in 1933, included all programs of the speech and drama department, which the Jaycee Masquers had not. Each year Guild members presented a series of one-act and three-act plays, provided speakers and readers to social and civic clubs throughout the city, and sponsored the Verse Speaking Choir, which performed at numerous community functions.[45] The school's music club and orchestra, under the direction of music instructor Laurence Powell, also performed at various public events.

Little Rockians gained an awareness of Jaycee in a less "refined" way as well. While the primary focus of the college remained a liberal arts program, in the late 1930s the effects of the Depression forced school officials to experiment with vocational training, and in 1938 they established their most extensive venture in this direction — a peanut butter plant run by students in a small facility on Fourteenth Street, under the direction of vocational instructor W.L. Travis and an advisory committee headed by Dean Brothers. Patterned on the Henry Ford Trade School at Dearborn, Michigan, the project taught the participants the fundamentals of scientific farming, production, and distribution. The college purchased peanuts from local farmers, converted them into peanut butter, and funneled all sales profits back into the project. The high school print shop provided jar labels bearing an outline of the state of Arkansas and the words "Build Arkansas — Use Jaycee Butter." School officials saw the entire experiment as an unusual combination of agriculture, education, industry, and science.[46] In 1939 the peanut butter factory relocated to a dairy on the Hot Springs Highway, but soon faded out of existence as a result of World War II and administrative decisions to deemphasize vocational training.

The entire era of the 1930s marked an increase in the school's commitment to community service. LRJC sponsored workshops and forums and provided cultural activities for the entire city. In addition, the administration and the faculty expanded Jaycee's curriculum to include adult education programs. In the early twentieth century, adult education usually denoted teaching language skills to illiterates and immigrants, but after the mid-1920s the new "people's colleges" initiated programs of evening classes or correspondence courses that offered older students the opportunity to enrich their lives or gain needed skills.

As early as 1935, LRJC conducted non-credit night courses in "Contemporary Continental Drama and Contemporary Novel."[47] Prior to World War II the school also provided adult education courses in family relations for young married couples, sketching, art history, and literature. These efforts by the instructors of the junior college and later the faculty of Little Rock University and the University of Arkansas at Little Rock to provide enrichment and other programs for the entire community became one of the institution's most significant contributions to the development of education in the state.

Members of the Jaycee community also participated in a variety of local events and activities. Many faculty members and administrators maintained active memberships in local civic and religious organizations and aided in charity drives like the Community Chest and the Red Feather campaign. In 1937 Jaycee students who belonged to the National Guard spent three weeks helping flood victims in northeast Arkansas, while three years later representatives from LRJC participated in a pioneering interracial meeting at Dunbar Junior College.[48]

One concern shared by many American undergraduates in the late 1930s was world peace. As war clouds gathered in Europe, students at Little Rock Junior College, like their counterparts on other campuses, promoted the peace movement. In a 1936 *Chatter* editorial on the civil war in Spain, one Jaycee writer wrote that "we who must be the soldiers in the next war should fight for peace."[49] The following spring the *College Chatter* and the LRJC Student Council sponsored a local strike for peace under the auspices of the National United Student Peace Committee. On that occasion Dean Brothers allowed Jaycee students to support the strike by leaving classes for one hour.[50]

After the outbreak of war in Europe in 1939, the campus paper and the International Relations Club energetically supported the national peace movement designed to keep the United States out of the conflict. "More power to the all-college peace front," one Jaycee campus editor wrote. "A million students will demonstrate that the Yanks are not coming to aid in the present imperialistic massacre in Europe."[51] As late as April 1940 a delegation of LRJC students participated in a series of peace demonstrations in opposition to American involvement in the war in Europe. While hardly radical in their political beliefs, these students did reflect the general isolationist view that characterized American public opinion in the early 1940s.

That sentiment changed dramatically both at Little Rock Junior College and in the nation as a whole following the Japanese attack on Pearl Harbor on December 7, 1941. After that, the reality of World War II dominated affairs on the campus and, in many ways, brought changes to the college that forever prevented a return to the leisurely atmosphere of the prewar era.

C H A P T E R   F I V E

From Pearl Harbor to Hayes Street, 1941-1949

*A*t 12:30, Monday, December 8, 1941 ... students jam the auditorium to hear the declaration of war by President Roosevelt. Everywhere there is a hushed silence and then suddenly a burst of applause as the President enters the Congressional chambers. Immediately following the declaration there is thunderous cheering and wild applause. "We'll make them remember Pearl Harbor! Down with the Nazis!"[1]

Norma Hyatt's account in the *College Chatter* of what happened at Little Rock Junior College the day following the Japanese attack on Pearl Harbor captured the emotional response of a generation that had reached a major turning point in their collective lives. Whether serving in the armed forces, working in defense industries, or suffering separation from or loss of loved ones, members of the Jaycee community experienced tremendous upheaval as a result of World War II. Moreover, the war had an impact on the institution itself, altering the structure of the student body, changing the curriculum, and, most importantly, ushering in an entire new era in the history of the college.

From the beginning of the conflict, the faculty and students of LRJC joined America's fighting forces and over the course of the war saw action in both Europe and the Pacific theaters. By May 1945, as the fighting drew to an end, the *College Chatter* included a full page with an eagle at the top above the words "Honor Roll." Below, the paper listed hundreds of Jaycee students, teachers, and alumni who served in the armed forces, including some names accompanied by an asterisk indicating "those who have made the supreme sacrifice for their country."[2]

While many members of the junior college community were on active military duty, the war also led to adjustments in the curriculum and certain programs there. Like most American colleges and universities, LRJC underwent radical changes during the mid-1940s, adding war-related courses, accelerating the regular schedules, and promoting fund-raising drives to help the country's military effort. At Jaycee, students tended to register for heavier course loads and to place greater emphasis on practical courses throughout the war years.

One of the most popular of these new areas of study was the Civilian Pilot Training Program, sponsored by LRJC and the Civil Aeronautics Authority. Established in 1939, the program included courses in flight theory, flight training, and cross-country flying, and offered a private pilot's license to students who completed the training. Government officials selected Jaycee over several larger schools as one of the first colleges to participate in CAA pilot education because of the facilities at Adams Field, Little Rock's civilian airport, and the availability of two competent professors — Lieutenant Edward Garbacz and Lieutenant Claude Holbart. Garbacz and Holbart each had extensive military service and flight experience and quickly made the LRJC program the largest flight training school in the state.[3]

Vera Hardcastle Greene, the LRJC librarian, supplemented the pilots' education program by establishing a branch library at Adams Field. The library proved to be an essential part of the training because the lack of time between flights precluded the men's using the library facilities at the main campus. At Greene's insistence the branch library included not only technical works but also novels and short stories about aviation and a volume of poems about flying.[4]

By 1941 the flight training program included over 60 male students, but school officials excluded women "due to their inability to undergo the strict training."[5] Men who completed the course usually went into the various branches of the armed forces that offered further flight training, and most of them served their country during the war as pilots or in related areas.

Little Rock Junior College offered other military opportunities as well. In October 1942 Dean Brothers announced the formation of a new offering in military arts. Taught by retired Army Colonel Harry B. Smith, the program stressed military principles, military drilling, and calisthenics in an effort to prepare LRJC students for service in the armed forces. By the end of the month over 80 percent of the male students at Jaycee had enrolled in the course.[6] The following spring the United States Navy Department accepted the school as a V-1 Accredited College, which allowed candidates to remain in college while completing preliminary work in areas like mathematics and physics before starting formal training to become naval officers.[7]

During World War II, in an effort to accelerate the institution's offerings to meet wartime needs, school officials altered the normal college calendar. In 1943 the faculty accepted a recommendation from Dean Brothers and President Larson to shorten the spring term by eliminating the regular examination week, in order to allow students to receive the maximum amount of college credit before entering the armed forces.[8] A year earlier, the LRJC faculty had also voted to grant full credit to every student called into military service before the conclusion of the semester by giving students the grade they had achieved in each course at the time of their induction.[9]

This quickening of the pace of education extended into the high schools. During the war, Jaycee officials allowed qualified students to omit their final year of secondary school and receive both a high school diploma and a year of college credit upon the completion of a year of studies at LRJC.[10] This experiment actually had a precedent at the college; in 1934 LRJC had allowed a select group of high school seniors to enroll at Jaycee, with outstanding results. The administration had discontinued the practice in 1936, but reinstituted the option because of the war. Several years later, college officials again inaugurated a program of admitting high school seniors when a crisis over racial integration forced the closing of the Little Rock public schools.

World War II affected extracurricular activities too. The *College Chatter* staff voluntarily submitted to censorship regulations imposed by the federal government. Most of these prohibited the mentioning of specific military units in combat areas or publishing the names of sailors and Marines in connection with their assigned ships and bases.[11] Although normally the guardians of a free press, American journalists readily abided by restrictions deemed essential to the war effort, and college reporters were no exception. In fact, all students seemed to be experiencing a new sense of purpose and responsibility because of the war. They had little time for nonessential activities. The campus paper noted the decline of card games in the Grill and on the lawn and a general reduction of "horseplay" in hallways and recreational areas. The editor of the *Chatter* summarized these changes by writing that "with war menacing the future of almost every home ... a great responsibility lies on the shoulders of those of us who are left at home. Our duty is to seek knowledge for the preservation of a civilization that is so rapidly being torn down by the ravages of hate."[12]

The college students of the 1940s shared this sense of purpose with the American public as a whole. Perhaps at no other time in American history did the citizens of the nation exhibit such prolonged feelings of unity. The Jaycee students during the war manifested this sense of commonality by participating in a variety of community service projects. When the government instituted a food rationing program, several LRJC coeds voluntarily worked in Little Rock grocery stores to explain the rationing to shoppers to ease the transition to the new and often confusing system.[13] Jaycee women also assisted in nationwide charity drives like the March of Dimes by collecting money in downtown Little Rock or soliciting funds on a door-to-door basis. The LRJC faculty also contributed to community events. For example, Mary Elizabeth Pape, a biology instructor, taught first aid classes for the Red Cross through a program sponsored by St. Vincent's Hospital.

Moreover, the Jaycee community contributed time and money to numerous war-related service projects. LRJC maintained a War Bond booth in the main hallway of the school during each major war loan drive and conducted competitions among the college clubs to increase sales. In one drive the school raised over $14,000 for the war through the efforts of social groups like the Battlecriers, Phi Alpha Beta, Delta Kappa, and Zeta Phi.[14] Organizations that failed to support the campaigns were chastised by the other students. In 1944 when one fraternity failed to contribute to a nationwide paper drive, a writer in the school newspaper pointed out to the entire campus that "the high and mighty Phi Alpha Betas, the cocky ones who ruled the social limelight until this year, have not contributed one, not one single pound of waste paper to the paper drive [and] ... should be publicly burned at the stake."[15]

Perhaps no LRJC group contributed more to the war on the homefront than the Battlecriers. Originally a booster club for Jaycee athletic teams, the Battlecriers evolved into a social sorority that maintained a sense of service. In addition to their annual financing of a campus beautification program, the Battlecriers sponsored benefit parties to raise money for comfort kits for American servicemen, filled cookie jars at the local USO, and purchased magazine subscriptions for military libraries. Many Battlecrier activities, while designed to aid the war effort, coincidentally afforded the college women a chance to meet the young servicemen stationed in the Little Rock area. On Sunday afternoons throughout the war, members of the Battlecriers served as "coke girls" at the USO snack bar, where they sold soft drinks, candy, and sandwiches. In 1944 the sorority went to Camp Robinson near North Little Rock to entertain convalescing soldiers with a musical show that included a routine called the "Blitzkreig Chorus."[16]

The Battlecriers' desire to meet young men was understandable, because the demands of war had drastically reduced the number of male students on the Little Rock Junior College campus. By 1944 slightly less than 40 percent of the Jaycee student body were men, and the female students felt the change. One coed in 1943 predicted that "sooner or later this institution will be manless. Girls will sit forlornly in the rec room or the Grill, reminiscing of the old days when there were men — ones who could grow whiskers — going to J.C."[17] If the war left many college girls lonely, the effects of the conflict also gave female students a new awareness of their own capabili-

ties. "This war is not only a young man's war," the editor of the 1943 *Chatter* wrote, "it is rapidly becoming a young woman's war also. No longer is the young woman expected to stay in the house, but now with the advent of this terrible war, has ... donned trousers to work in the factories ... and in the fields."[18] Such feminist expression, encouraged by wartime circumstances, was stymied in the 1950s and early 1960s but eventually blossomed into one of the most significant social movements in recent American history.

In the early 1940s, when the war's outcome remained in doubt, news of battlefield reverses in Europe and the Pacific generated hysteria on the LRJC campus. Although fully aware of Arkansas's location in the interior of the United States, far from any coast, college officials issued reams of instructions informing students of elaborate procedures to follow in case either Japanese bombers or the German Luftwaffe should initiate a bombing raid against the citizens of central Arkansas. School officials told students if they heard the school bell ring repeatedly they should "gather around the inside walls of the first floor." Under no circumstances, the faculty told their charges, were students to go to the gymnasium or the upstairs of the main building because "the thin structure of the roofs would not offer much resistance to any type of bomb." Finally school leadership reassured the student body that "the men in Military Drill classes are responsible for incendiary bomb protection."[19]

In spite of wartime hysteria and other changes brought by American involvement in World War II, many day-to-day campus activities went on as usual. Students celebrated Donaghey Day, elected May Queens, gathered in the Grill, attended classes, and studied for exams. According to the *Chatter* a larger percentage of LRJC undergraduates than ever before worked their way through school during the mid-1940s because of labor shortages caused by the war and employers' willingness to bend schedules to accommodate students. One Jaycee student of the era, Orville Henry, forged a lifetime career from part-time employment. Exempt from the draft because he was underweight, Henry wrote a sports column for the *Chatter* and served as the part-time sports editor of the *Arkansas Gazette*. When the *Gazette*'s regular sports editor accepted other employment, the paper promoted the nineteen-year-old Henry to the job.[20] Henry remained in the position for 40 years, becoming a highly visible figure in the state's athletic world as a sportswriter and uncritical promoter of the athletic program at the University of Arkansas at Fayetteville.

Between 1941 and 1945, the LRJC campus changed in many ways — military-oriented courses, a high ratio of women students, a younger student body, a new emphasis on community service — but the major impact of World War II on Little Rock Junior College came after the war with an unprecedented rush by war veterans to acquire an education. Aided by the provisions of the federal "G.I. Bill," which granted tuition payments and subsistence allowances, thousands of American war veterans enrolled in institutions of higher education throughout the nation, straining facilities like Jaycee to the limit.

At LRJC the editor of the *Trojan* called 1947 the year when "khaki and navy blue have been exchanged for plaid shirts and tweed suits, when campaign ribbons have been exchanged for fraternity pins ...."[21] Due to the sudden influx of veterans during the years immediately after World War II, classes met six days a week and the school more than doubled the number of faculty members from 22 to 45. Through the efforts of John Larson, LRJC acquired five temporary buildings from Camp Robinson to provide additional classrooms, a cafeteria, and a recreational lounge and, according to a promotional pamphlet from the early 1950s, despite the number of GIs, "no veteran was turned away from Jaycee for lack of room."

During war years the college's average enrollment remained steady at around 250 students, but in the fall of 1946 it leaped to over 800. Where only a year before female students outnumbered males three to one, the GIs reversed that ratio, and by 1951 enrollment reached an all-time high of over 1350 students with a faculty of 52.[22]

The veterans affected campus life in diverse ways. One undergraduate remarked that "in the past a student could take his time and leisurely walk from one class to the other, while today there is such a crowd and such confusion when the bell rings."[23] The GIs also dominated campus politics for several years, starting with the 1946 election for student body president. That year Cleveland Harrison and Robert Wallace received the routine nomination from the nominating committee appointed by Dean Brothers. When Wallace withdrew, under usual school procedure, Harrison would have won by default. Rebelling against tradition, however, the LRJC Veterans Organization held a mass meeting on campus and nominated Roger Howard to oppose Harrison. Both candidates had served during the war — Harrison as an Army infantryman and Howard in the Navy — and in a record voter turnout, Howard defeated Harrison. The race caused one longtime faculty member to comment, "[T]here is more student interest in today's presidential election than ever shown before."[24] Howard's victory symbolized the GIs' impact on the traditional operation of the college.

The *Chatter* attempted to accommodate the veterans with a special column called "Strictly GI," which contained news and articles on matters like GI insurance and GI home loans. The presence of so many older, more mature students gave the college a tone of seriousness and sense of purpose, in addition to a certain worldliness that at times disturbed the administration. For instance, Dean Brothers worried that younger students might be lured into the poker and crap games that the veterans persisted in playing, and he repeatedly threatened to close the recreation room if the gambling continued.[25] Despite this minor difficulty, faculty members and administrators generally felt the veterans had a positive impact on Little Rock Junior College. One instructor later recalled that the GIs "were mature young people, and they did an awful lot to help the school. Some became great supporters of the college."[26]

If the GIs helped the school, Jaycee reciprocated, not only by offering the education the veterans desired, but also by providing needed auxiliary services. Between 1946 and 1952 the Little Rock Junior College Guidance Center helped hundreds of veterans to determine their capabilities and set realistic educational and vocational objectives. The Veterans' Administration had inadequate resources to meet the needs of the returning soldiers and sailors in 1946, and the Guidance Center at LRJC, like similar programs throughout the country, cooperated with the federal government to fill the gap. The college received $20.65 from the VA for each veteran counseled and in turn provided a professional staff, which at the height of the program in March 1950 processed over 300 veterans.[27]

While the veterans changed the nature of campus life at Little Rock Junior College in the late 1940s, their most important impact was on the school's future development, for starting in 1946 they actively promoted the concept of expanding the school into a four-year institution. The GIs spoke to civic and other groups and gave radio programs encouraging the community to develop a complete collegiate program in the capital city. Their aspirations resurrected the old vision of a municipal university that so many early supporters of LRJC had had, and although the school did not make the transition to a four-year college for almost a dozen more years, the GIs' rekindling of that idea proved to be the stimulus that eventually resulted in Little Rock University.

While LRU remained a distant dream, the overcrowding of the buildings at Thirteenth and State presented an immediate problem to the LRJC administration. The unexpected influx of war veterans created an almost intolerable situation in terms of classroom space, laboratories, and library facilities. Seeing no room for expansion at the Thirteenth and State site, school officials decided to move the institution to what they hoped would be a permanent home.

As early as November 1946, when the first wave of GIs enrolled at the school, President Larson recognized that the campus would be inadequate to meet the school's future needs. In a memo to Dean Brothers, Larson wrote that "there is no question LRJC is in desperate need of new quarters ... [we] should make some provision either for a minimum site of 4 city blocks within the city or a larger site in the general line of the city's growth."[28] That same month the Little Rock School Board selected a site committee to investigate relocating the college, and by January 1947 expanded the group to include Charles Thompson, William Nash, William Steinkamp, Werner Knoop, James H. Penick, Alfred Kahn, and LRJC President John Larson.[29]

The Site Committee initially recommended the purchase of a tract of land on the Hot Springs highway, but several members of the school board expressed reservations that the location might be too far from the downtown area, which they regarded as the "hub of the city."[30] A few weeks after rejecting the highway property the school board indicated the members favored purchasing acreage owned by Mr. and Mrs. Dan Cammack, near Cammack Village in the northern sector of the city. The 58-acre tract carried a purchase price of $125,000, but Cammack agreed to wave $25,000 as a gift to the college. But even a $100,000 price tag made a few of the board members hesitate.[31]

In the meantime, the Site Committee continued to investigate other possible localities. For example, they considered a 40-acre tract between West Sixteenth and West Twentieth Streets that had been suggested in a series of correspondence between M. LaFayette Harris, the president of Philander Smith College, an all-black Methodist institution, and James H. Penick. Harris expressed an interest in his college's acquiring LRJC's Thirteenth and State campus and asked Penick to consider the property on Sixteenth Street, which had been purchased 20 years earlier as a future site for Philander Smith. Harris informed Penick that the leadership of his college no longer considered the location suitable for Philander Smith's needs because a move would "jeopardize jobs near downtown and ... most significant of all, the neighborhood in which the property is located is becoming a white neighborhood. I persuaded the Trustees that we should remain where we are, rather than run the risk of incurring ill will from many white citizens."[32] The Philander Smith campus lay only a block away from LRJC's Thirteenth and State location, and Harris reminded Penick that "the colored people are pushing out around Little Rock Junior College with all indications that the entire community will be a Negro community very soon."[33]

Initially Penick rejected Harris's overtures and informed him that the school board had "put Little Rock Junior College on notice that they will need the building [at Thirteenth and State] for the 1947 term for the use of pupils in that area."[34] Although the school board had no such intention, Penick did express interest in acquiring the property between West Sixteenth and West Twentieth Streets as a possible new location for LRJC.[35] Ironically, Jaycee officials

*Raymond Rebsamen, prominent Little
Rock businessman who donated the original
80-acre site on Hayes Street that became the
campus of LRJC, LRU, and UALR. (Arkansas History Commission — Thomas Harding
Photo Collection)*

eventually found another location for the college and the Little Rock School Board sold the Thirteenth and State property to Philander Smith, which generated some of the ill will the Philander Smith president had wished to avoid. In a letter to the Little Rock School Board, Joe H. Bilheimer, a local property owner, protested "the sale of the present Junior College site at 13th and State ... to any person or persons, or any school or college to be used by the negroes." Bilheimer also submitted a petition signed by over 600 white residents who objected to the purchase, claiming that if Philander Smith acquired the site the sale would "ruin more than a million dollars' worth of property."[36]

The West Sixteenth property owned by Philander Smith proved too small for the needs of Little Rock Junior College. Although several members of the Site Committee grew impatient as the search for a new campus continued, Larson insisted that someday LRJC would expand to a four-year institution that would require a spacious campus. In the spring of 1947 his patience was rewarded when Raymond Rebsamen, a Little Rock business executive, generously donated an 80-acre tract of land on Hayes Street to Little Rock Junior College. The location provided ample space close to downtown yet secluded in an attractive wooded area. Although part of the land rested on low ground that presented drainage problems, Larson insisted that the first buildings be built on that part of the site in order to "leave the good land for the great university which was to come."[37] Following Rebsamen's gift the move to the new campus came in phases. As early as the fall term of 1947, school officials secured four temporary

buildings from the Stuttgart airfield and offered courses in physics, biology, and chemistry at the Hayes Street location. The classrooms faced south on 32nd Street in an area that did not interfere with the construction of permanent buildings, and students and faculty used a makeshift entrance from Fair Park Boulevard.[38] By 1949 the campus had expanded to twelve semi-permanent buildings acquired from various military installations, which the college used for classrooms, laboratories, a bookstore, a library, and a cafeteria. Through the cooperation of the local utility companies and the City of Little Rock, gas, electric, telephone, water, and sewer services "were extended to Jaycee at a minimum outlay of college funds."[39]

Next the leadership of LRJC faced the task of raising funds for permanent buildings. Because the laws of Arkansas still specifically prohibited the levy of school tax money for institutions beyond the twelfth grade, and because the Donaghey Foundation charter granted revenue to the school for operating purposes only, Jaycee officials had to turn to the citizens of Little Rock for the necessary support to relocate. The resulting campaign not only produced the desired revenue but also created an atmosphere of common purpose between the community and the college that lasted for over 20 years. To conduct the fund-raising drive, a group of interested business and professional people created a non-profit corporation called the Little Rock Junior College Foundation. Under the general chairmanship of James H. Penick, the president of Worthen Bank and Trust Company, the foundation launched the "Permanent Home Campaign" to raise $755,000 to finance the construction of a modern campus on the Hayes Street site. The directors of the Little Rock School Board served as ex-officio members of the foundation, assuring necessary coordination with the school's governing body, and beginning in early 1948 the Permanent Home Campaign, according to one official, became "one of the most successful money-raising ventures in the history of Little Rock and North Little Rock."[40]

The solicitation officially started on February 3, 1948, with a "Kick-Off Dinner" at the Marion Hotel. Congressman Brooks Hays delivered the main address to a large gathering of group chairmen, division leaders, team captains, and other workers and supporters. "An adequate modern plant for Little Rock Junior College will mean more to the future progress and prosperity of the Little Rock area than any other single enterprise of which I can conceive," Hays told the audience. "I consider this project the most important civic undertaking ever launched in the history of Greater Little Rock."[41]

To promote the drive, directors of the Permanent Home Campaign tried to sell the college to the community as a business investment. One piece of literature informed readers that "LRJC is the equivalent of an established industry with a payroll of $1,000,000 a year ... [T]he faculty and students put upwards of $967,645 into Greater Little Rock trade channels. LRJC is Good Business. It is *Big* Business."[42] A task force of speakers to civic and other community organizations also stressed the economic value of the services of Jaycee graduates to local businesses and industries. While this approach unquestionably helped raise the needed funds for the buildings, the promises of economic benefits placed the expansion of the college on the same level as the establishment of a new factory — a means of creating employment and circulating money in the community. LRJC, however, served different purposes than a factory. By representing the school as an economic venture the members of the foundation created an unfortunate popular image of Jaycee as some kind of training facility to serve the economic goals of the area. Yet general education remained the core of the school's curriculum, and the narrow business-oriented concept plagued LRJC's efforts to upgrade the school's liberal arts programs for several years following the Permanent Home Campaign.

Spokesmen for the drive did point out that the rural sections of Pulaski County would benefit from the establishment of an improved campus because LRJC offered many youths from these areas the only locally available college work, and without the school those students "might otherwise have to curtail their education with the completion of the high school years."[43] Community pride became another focus of the campaign. Workers reminded potential donors that Little Rock might be the only city of its size in the country that did not have a permanently housed institution of higher education and promised that if the drive succeeded the capital city would have a junior college plant unsurpassed in the South.

To raise money for the new buildings the Little Rock Junior College Foundation relied on a tightly structured organization. Under Penick's directorship, K.A. Engel, publisher of the *Arkansas Democrat*, and W.R. Crow, president of the Crow-Burlingame Company, co-chaired the Pattern Gifts Committee which solicited gifts of $5000 or more. Other committees included a General Solicitation Section, a Special Gifts Section, and a Campus and Alumni Section. Dr. Granville Davis, a history instructor at the college, headed the campus group that contacted graduates and former Jaycee students. Davis had been among the first graduates of LRJC and had earned the distinction of being the first alumnus to earn a doctor of philosophy degree. His efforts on behalf of the Permanent Home Campaign also contributed to his selection as president of the college a few years later.

Although generally successful, the Permanent Home Campaign disgruntled some members of the local business community. The president of Little Rock's Union National Bank wrote to the campaign director and expressed "shock at seeing the $3000 contribution of Worthen Bank to the Junior College Fund," claiming that the donation violated a previous agreement against such gifts.[44] The president of Commercial National Bank wrote to the bank's stockholders informing them that he opposed the bank's making a direct contribution to the Little Rock Junior College Foundation as many other businesses had done, preferring that individual shareholders give whatever they wished.[45]

Despite these inevitable disagreements, the aggressive campaign brought the desired results. Not only did the Little Rock business community as a whole generously support the drive, but people who had left the community also donated. The president of the First National Bank in St. Louis, Missouri, a former Little Rock resident, wrote to

Penick: "I know of nothing that is more deserving of support than the campaign to provide a permanent home for LRJC. For this reason, I am breaking what has necessarily become a rule with me [against giving to causes outside the St. Louis area] and I am sending you a check ...."[46] Over two years after the official close of the Permanent Home Campaign, volunteers continued to solicit past due balances on pledges made during the drive. This kind of tireless effort caused one *Arkansas Gazette* writer to comment that the Little Rock Junior College Foundation had "conducted the largest and most successful financial campaign of its kind that Little Rock had seen."[47]

One of the most important long-range effects of the Permanent Home Campaign was the reorganization of the Little Rock Junior College Foundation on a full-time basis. The original 21 members increased to 75 and the membership established a board of trustees to serve staggered terms in overseeing the activities of the foundation. Penick served as president of the group while Engel acted as secretary-treasurer. The involvement of so many citizens in the foundation futher cemented the ties between the community and the college, and for the next 20 years Little Rock Junior College and later Little Rock University functioned as an institution backed by strong local support. Since the original Permanent Home Campaign raised only $650,000 of the $755,000 goal, the first activity of the revised foundation involved soliciting the remainder of the needed money, a task successfully completed by the end of 1948.

With the money raised by the Little

The South Building on the new campus in 1949. (UALR Archives Photo Collection 2, #3)

The arcade of LRJC's North Building. (UALR Archives Photo Collection 2, #7)

The John A. Larson Memorial Library. (UALR Archives Photo Collection 2, #10)

Rock Junior College Foundation, Jaycee officials built four modern buildings on the Hayes Street campus — two classroom buildings, a library, and a field house. Originally called the North Building and the South Building, the new classroom facilities contained ample instructional space as well as offices for the faculty, and their unique, modern design merited a feature article in *Progressive Architecture* magazine.[48]

Despite the success of the campaign and the construction of the modern campus, the late 1940s were also marked by tragedy at Jaycee. As the new campus neared completion in November 1949, President Larson died. In the two years preceding his death Larson had resigned as the principal of Little Rock Senior High School and devoted all his efforts to expanding the junior college, personally supervising much of the move to the new site. In a letter to the school board he wrote, "I have stood for rich scholarship and the enrichment of the lives of the young people ... I hope that the results speak for themselves."[49]

Almost immediately after Larson's death, the trustees of the college voted to name the new library in his honor. According to one writer, Larson had always regarded the library as the main focus of the college and spent many hours "walking over the newly broken campus talking about what the library would be like."[50] Although Larson objected to naming buildings after living people, on one occasion he publicly stated that if the board wished to so honor him posthumously, "if I should be given my choice I would choose the library."[51]

In the minds of many Little Rock citizens, John Larson personified the work that went on at Little Rock Junior College, and his death left an important legacy for higher education in the community. In a memorial statement James Penick said, "[A]s long as any of the buildings stand on the new LRJC campus a large debt of gratitude will still be owed to John Larson for the many years of unselfish labor and devotion he gladly gave to the cause of ... junior college education."[52] A student writer added in a later editorial that "as students come to the portals of the college ... the name John A. Larson will become legend ... [T]he Library will bear his name."[53]

The death of the college's president and founder, combined with the influx of GIs and the relocation of the institution from Thirteenth and State to the new Hayes Street location, signified the beginning of a new era at Jaycee. For many students and faculty members the late 1940s and early 1950s consequently came to be regarded as a "golden age" in the history of Little Rock Junior College. Following World War II the school entered a period of maturity — a new campus, a larger student body, an expanded curriculum, greater emphasis on student activities — and during that era John Larson's dream took a giant step toward becoming a modern college.

Registration line at Little Rock Junior College in 1949. (UALR Archives Photo Collection 2, #26)

Student Life in the Golden Age, 1947-1957

"*S*omewhere between general literacy and the training of specialists, there is a gap in American education.... The great army of U.S. industry has plenty of foot-soldiers and a trained high command, but lacks competent non-commissioned officers. Junior colleges supply this need." Appearing in the *Kiplinger Magazine* in 1947, this quotation reflected the popular perception of the American junior college in the post-World War II era. In Little Rock Junior College's last decade as a two-year institution — between 1947 and 1957 — LRJC educated those "non-commissioned officers" in record numbers. No longer the struggling little enterprise that conducted classes in the north wing of the high school and yet years from being a municipal university, LRJC experienced a decade of quality service and scholarship as a two-year institution. It offered smaller classes than most four-year schools, stressed individual attention for students, and promoted the democratization of higher education in central Arkansas.

The Jaycee students of the era tended to be typical of undergraduates at two-year institutions. Between 1950 and 1954 their median scores on the American College Examination fell in the 40th percentile, with slightly lower scores on

other national achievement tests.[1] By the mid-1950s, school officials indicated that most LRJC freshmen had the academic skills to do college-level work, and in 1956 the annual President's Report concurred, adding that "in a dynamic, urban society competition among students in the larger high schools ... gives students adequate preparation for success in college."[2] For these freshmen, Jaycee's appeal remained essentially what it had been when the school opened in 1927. "At a small school like LRJC," one student said in 1956, "you get to know almost everybody and you get to take part in a lot of activities that you'd miss in a big school. You can live at home and save money."[3]

Many LRJC alumni who attended the institution during its last decade as a junior college retained fond memories of campus life and social activities. For those connected with the college in 1949, one particular series of events reached legendary proportions and even placed LRJC in the national spotlight for a brief moment. In 1947 John Larson and other school officials had decided to restore intercollegiate football to the campus. They reached this decision after determining that the absence of a team injured student morale. A year earlier the editor of the *Chatter* had written that the

*A Trojan cheerleader during the 1947 football season. (1948 **Trojan**)*

"fall sports outlook is the same as usual, neither bright nor optimistic,"[4] and in February 1947 another student writer commented that "sports is not one of the leading activities around Jaycee. After bridge, dancing, eating, and perhaps studying, sports puts in a trembling appearance."[5] The lack of a football team also left Jaycee out of the mainstream of college life in Arkansas in the post-World War II era. As talented prewar grid stars returned to various schools in the late 1940s, the interest in football in the state soared. By the 1946 season both Hendrix College in Conway and College of the Ozarks in Clarksville had reestablished football programs, Arkansas Tech at Russellville had become a small college powerhouse, and the University of Arkansas Razorbacks under coach John Barnhill had aroused statewide interest in the school's football team.

Little Rock Junior College had not underwritten a complete athletic program since 1935, but in March 1947 Dean Brothers announced that beginning in the fall of that year Jaycee would again field a football team. Even before school authorities had named a coach, the students responded to the idea with considerable enthusiasm, culminating in an impromptu assembly of the whole student body in the gymnasium to organize a booster club. Soon afterwards T-shirts bearing the Trojan emblem became a leading sales item in the campus bookstore, and speculation concerning the new Trojans' gridiron fortunes became a favorite topic of conversation throughout the college community.[6]

In late April 1947, President Larson named James T. Karam as the new football coach and athletic director at Little Rock Junior College. A native of Lake Village, Arkansas, and a graduate of Auburn University in Alabama, where he played halfback on the football team, Karam had served in the United States Navy during World War II and, as part of his military service, had coached the North Island, Coronado, California, football team to a fleet air wing championship.[7] By May 1947 Karam had assembled a 45-man LRJC squad for spring practices, which he conducted on the football field at West Side Junior High School.

The resurrection of the football program at Jaycee resulted largely from the efforts of John Larson. The LRJC president had played football, basketball, and soccer during his college days and believed that an active sports program not only helped promote school spirit, but also aided in publicizing the work of the college. Karam later told an interviewer that Larson "was determined to have a football team and [was responsible] for hiring me. Only Larson's great tenacity and his love for kids kept that [program] going."[8]

In terms of establishing a winning tradition, the choice of Jimmy Karam as the school's first postwar football coach proved to be an excellent one. The college had no athletic dormitory, had a miniscule football budget, and offered no scholarships to players. Fortunately for the team, however, Karam had a streak of P.T. Barnum in him. "I'd go around town," the coach later recalled, "and Mr. Jim Penick at the Worthen Bank and Mr. [J.H.] Heiskill at the *Arkansas Gazette* and very prominent people in town would give me money to have the boys eat at a training table and help them some."[9]

Trojan Spirit — the campus bookstore, ca. 1950. (UALR Archives Photo Collection 2, #22)

Just how much "help" the football players received remained a mystery even to the school's top administrators. For three years Karam ran the football program on his own, and few people at LRJC questioned his methods because his teams won most of their games. Soon after his arrival the coach had acquired a war surplus building that served as a dormitory. By 1949 the facility housed 24 players, who made the 7:15 a.m. bus ride to Sullivan's boarding-house for breakfast and later dined at Sullivan's for lunch and dinner.[10]

In their inaugural season, Karam's Trojans rode a winning record to the Coffee Bowl in Coffeyville, Kansas, where they defeated the Coffeyville Junior College Red Ravens 31-7 before a crowd of over 5000 fans on Thanksgiving Day. The *College Chatter* reported that for a brief time during the year the Trojans ranked second in scoring among the nation's junior colleges and praised the team for placing the college in the public spotlight. "JC received much favorable publicity," one writer reported. "The state sat up and took notice."[11] After returning from Coffeyville, the members of the team received letter sweaters and Coffee Bowl awards from Arkansas governor Ben Laney at an all-school assembly.

In 1948, Karam's second year, the Trojans went 7-3 before losing an 18-7 decision to South Georgia Junior College in the Junior Sugar Bowl in Monroe, Louisiana. Earlier in the season, over 5,000 spectators watched the Trojans drop a 14-0 decision to the University of Arkansas freshman team in the first night game in Little Rock's new War Memorial Stadium.[12]

The following season marked the pinnacle of Little Rock Junior College athletic achievement, following a storybook script that might have been written in Hollywood. In September 1949 the campus paper reported that the "members of the Trojan football team formed their first important line-up of the season across Coleman Creek, in a successful attempt to save three small children marooned in a tree by a flash flood."[13] A torrent of rushing water had separated two young boys and a girl from their mother, who had rushed to the nearby college in search of help. Several members of the football squad were attending a team meeting and ran to the creek where they formed a human chain to transport the children back to land and then wrapped them in blankets until police and firemen arrived.

Less than a month later, the Trojans shattered a sixteen-game winning streak of the University of Arkansas freshman team by defeating the Shoats 34-0 in War Memorial Stadium. Jaycee continued to win, and as the season progressed the team attended a variety of social functions in their honor — like the cheeseburger supper given by Zeta Phi sorority, which included a songfest with a solo by Coach Karam.[14] With continuing success, the 1949 homecoming festivities at LRJC marked one of the major highlights of the season. Students held a bonfire and pep rally on the campus and then paraded through downtown Little Rock. The football team defeated Arkansas College 70-12 in the annual homecoming game and then the students proceeded to a dance at the Women's City Club that featured a grand march with the girls of the homecoming court and their football player escorts.

*Jimmy Karam, coach of Jaycee's 1949
Junior Rose Bowl Championship team. (1950*
Trojan)

The Trojans won ten straight games in 1949 (see the Appendix for a list of opponents and scores), garnering national recognition for the college. Part of the team's success resulted from the extreme confidence exhibited by the LRJC coach. Unlike most coaches, who recite a boring pregame litany of cautious clichés to the press, Karam usually predicted victory by a wide margin. Before one important game in 1949 he told reporters that "if we didn't have the best junior college team in the nation, they might beat us, but since we have, we'll beat them by four or five touchdowns. Jaycee has been called the Junior College Notre Dame … champions never have an off day, and we are champions."[15] That same day the Trojans defeated Northeast Center College of Louisiana by a score of 50-13.

To climax the 1949 football season, LRJC received an invitation to play in the Junior Rose Bowl in Pasadena, California — the most prestigious postseason junior college game in the nation. The bid silenced some of Karam's critics, who had expressed anger that Jaycee did not play enough Arkansas teams to compete for a state championship. For his part Karam maintained he had "bigger things in mind,"[16] and when he arrived in Little Rock with a police escort from Fayetteville, where he had been recruiting, following the announcement of the bowl bid, students, boosters, and sportswriters all applauded the coach's earlier decision.

Backed by local businessmen like J.S. Bailey, Lee Rogers, and P.C. Brown, the Trojans journeyed to California in December 1949 to meet Santa Anna Junior College before 50,000 people in the Junior Rose Bowl.[17] Arriving several days before the game, the team toured Hollywood movie studios, met several radio and motion picture stars, and attended a professional football game with tickets purchased by a group of ex-Arkansans who lived in southern California. Little Rock native and popular movie star Dick Powell spent a good deal of time with the team and even visited the dressing room at halftime of the game.[18]

The Trojans also received enthusiastic support from both the college community and other citizens of Little Rock. The Delta Kappa fraternity chartered a bus that took 50 students to the game, and the *Arkansas Gazette* and the Rebsamen-East Insurance Company sponsored a radio broadcast of the contest for Trojan fans in Arkansas.

The Trojans' starting line-up for the Junior Rose Bowl included Joe Shinn, Louis Waldron, Bill Forte, Harry Denson, James Shenick, Bob Sullenger, and Shelby Helmbeck in the line and Harold (Tiger) Waggoner, George Roberts, Ralph Troillett, and O'Neal Wilkerson in the starting backfield. Under the leadership of quarterback Troillett, the overall play of Waggoner, and an 85-yard punt return by Benny Scott, Little Rock Junior College defeated Santa Ana 25-19, to cap the greatest football season in the school's history.

For all the hoopla and excitement surrounding the 1949 Junior Rose Bowl, LRJC realized a paltry $1,364 above expenses for participating in the game, and received that money only after filing a lawsuit against bowl officials in California.[19] But the college gained a tremendous amount of public recognition for playing in the bowl. It had always suffered identity problems, and its nationally successful athletic team generated

The 1949 Trojan football team that beat Santa Ana College for the championship of the Junior Rose Bowl. (1950 **Trojan)**

Part of the hoopla surrounding the Trojans' win in the 1949 Junior Rose Bowl in California. (1950 **Trojan***)*

*LRJC students enjoying the snow and each other. (1951 **Trojan**)*

a positive image that lasted well into the 1950s. In December 1949 voters selected the LRJC coach as "Little Rockian of the Year." In his typically blunt manner Karam later boasted that "nobody ever heard of Little Rock Junior College 'til we had football. We were just a little school stuck out here and nobody had ever heard of it. Football put it on the map. At that time we were the football team in the state ... so the whole state was behind us."[20] For several years after the game, LRJC's business manager continued to receive requests from high schools and civic groups for the film of the Junior Rose Bowl game. In 1953 a local businessman wrote to Foster Vineyard, a member of the school's board of trustees: "I think all will agree that the golden era of Karam's fine teams did more for the college than any other one thing."[21]

Much of the positive publicity for the school stemmed from Karam's promotion of his team as a group of unwanted overachievers. "My kids were kids that couldn't make it at other colleges," he later recalled. "These were kids who wanted an education, they wanted to go to college, they wanted to get a degree ... [T]hey were good workers, fine clean students."[22] In building a national gridiron power at LRJC, however, Karam encountered difficulties in subsidizing Trojan athletes. As late as 1986 one longtime member of the board of trustees, in discussing campus housing, referred to the dormitory "that housed the semi-pro team that won the J.C. Bowl [in 1949]."[23]

The year before the Junior Rose Bowl the *College Chatter* ran a satirical article suggesting that the subsidy question could be solved simply by publishing what each player received in the weekly game reports. "Now John Hestir ($45 per month) heaves a long pass to Shelby Helmbeck ($35 plus room and board). Helmbeck fumbles, but Joe Shinn ($30 per month plus the use of Coach Karam's car) recovers ...."[24]

During the fall of 1949 President Larson wrote to Manning M. Pattillo of the North Central Association, expressing concern that the college might be endangering the institution's accreditation by subsidizing athletes. "Our problem," Larson wrote, "seems to be that of doing what certain interests deem necessary to hold certain students in college competition with other colleges in the state in football."[25] Pattillo informed Larson that "athletes should not be favored above other students in such matters as the distribution of scholarships, loan funds, grants of financial aid...."[26] Partly as a result of this conflict, Jimmy Karam resigned as the football coach at Little Rock Junior College to enter private business. Members of the administration and the school board, wanting to uphold the academic integrity of the institution, refused Karam's demand that he maintain total control of the football program,[27] and the coach and the college severed relations on an amiable basis. Karam said at the time, "I was happy working here at J.C. I am glad to have had a part in reviving athletics here."[28] The Trojans' former leader went on to become a successful Little Rock merchant, while Jaycee athletics stagnated over the ensuing years until the institution dropped varsity football and basketball in the mid-1950s.

While football provided a unifying element in the late forties and early fifties, the LRJC students participated in a wide variety of other activities. The adminis-

The Donaghey Day luncheon at the Marion Hotel in 1950. (UALR Archives Photo Collection 2, #50)

tration supported these extracurricular events out of a conviction that the college had an obligation to do more for the welfare of the student body than provide academic instruction. "A college is known by the type of students it trains," Dean Brothers commented in 1953. "An educational institution may be rich in endowment, possess magnificent buildings, and have a faculty with the finest training, but if the students it turns out ... have not shown growth and development ... then something has been neglected."[29] This attitude reflected a popular conception in higher educational circles that the institution had a responsibility to encourage students' physical, social, and spiritual growth along with training their minds. Consequently the LRJC administration and faculty worked with the student council, various service organizations, and social, recreational, and academic interest clubs to develop a well-rounded group of undergraduates.

For a few years in the early 1950s the college had a marching band. Responding to the football team's success, the band performed at LRJC games dressed in distinctive uniforms of maroon shirts, blue jeans, confederate caps, and white throat scarves.

In 1952 the administration restructured LRJC's student government system to enhance student involvement in college affairs. Responding to student complaints of inadequate representation in the Student Council, school officials inaugurated the new and distinctive Student Government Association, which included a president elected by the entire student body; a male and female representative from each class; and representatives from each council in proportion to the size of the various academic areas. Students selected representatives from the Liberal Arts Council, the Business Council, the Engineering Council, the Practical Arts Council, and the Medical Council. A year after the inauguration of the new system, the Business Council, with almost 200 members, became the largest of the councils, indicating the increasing popularity of commercial training over liberal arts education in the early 1950s.[30] Despite the reorganization of the system, the Student Government Association remained a conservative organization throughout the decade. Often criticized for inaction by other students, the members of the SGA avoided controversial areas and tended to carry out the wishes of the faculty and administration, until the 1960s when a new and more militant generation of students became involved in the campus governing process.

LRJC's Phi Theta Kappa chapter continued to play a significant role in the national junior college's honorary activities. In 1954 it hosted the organization's national convention at the Marion Hotel in downtown Little Rock, where Jimmy Kendrick, the president of the local chapter, and Ernest Lawrence, the president of the Little Rock Junior College student body, chaired the meeting.[31] Throughout the school's existence as a two-year institution, LRJC maintained one of Phi Theta Kappa's most active and energetic chapters, providing Little Rock undergraduates the opportunity to work with junior college students from other parts of the country.

The *College Chatter*, another traditional Jaycee institution, also flourished in the first half of the decade, winning recognition in 1954 as the best college news-

*LRJC social life in 1953. (1953 **Trojan**)*

paper in the state, under the editorship of Bill Sims. Despite such honors, campus newspapers like the *Chatter* often encountered criticism from other students. In the late 1940s the editor of the *Chatter* ran a perceptive editorial defending the efforts of collegiate journalists. "If we print jokes, people say we are silly," the editor wrote. "If we don't they say we are snobbish; if we clip things from other papers, we're too lazy to write them ourselves; if we don't we're too fond of our own stuff; if we print gossip we step on somebody's toes; if we don't the paper's dull."[32] Because of the influence of Wisconsin senator Joseph McCarthy and his accusations of communist infiltration of American life, college writers in the early 1950s, like other citizens, tended to avoid political issues and activities and shied away from controversial attitudes out of a fear of being labeled un-American. Undergraduates sought security through conformity. At LRJC, opinion polls indicated most student concerns centered on campus parking, improving the registration process at the school, and securing a job after graduation rather than national and international issues. On April 8, 1954, however, the editor of the *College Chatter* defied the conventional wisdom and ran the paper's only editorial of the era that commented on the impact of the "red-baiting" of the decade. "Our colleges are being invaded by an atmosphere of fear and suppression created by irresponsible investigators, hysterical community leaders and other self-appointed thought police," the article said. "[Those people] have succeeded in intimidating both our students and faculties [who] are afraid to ask questions on controversial subjects or sup-

port unpopular causes."[33] After the appearance of that single courageous editorial, the *Chatter* returned to reporting student elections and parties, sports events, and other non-controversial activities. If Jaycee students publicly supported unpopular causes or expressed opinions on the political events of the day, those matters never appeared in the *College Chatter*. Still, generations of Jaycee students relied on the paper for information concerning campus activities, sports events, and student opinion, and journalism students gained valuable work experience in publishing it.

Physical education students had opportunities for career practice as well. For several years they coached interscholastic teams and supervised recreational activities for children in grades one through six in the Little Rock School District.[34]

In the early 1950s, under the direction of LRJC graduate Cleveland Harrison, the Trojan Theater Guild presented four three-act plays each year. In 1953 it joined with the Little Rock Parent-Teacher Association in a production of *The Wizard of Oz* for the children of the local public schools and donated the proceeds from the play to a scholarship fund for Jaycee students.

This same spirit of aiding the college reached new heights with the 1954 Campus Clean-up Campaign. On April 20, the administration dismissed classes and "students swarmed over the campus to gather up paper, sticks, and other unsightly debris."[35] Unfortunately, for many years student effort proved insufficient to acquire a much-needed bridge over Coleman Creek on the eastern border of the campus, which, when swollen by rain, created havoc for Jaycee

A LRJC dance in 1950. (UALR Archives Photo Collection 2, #62)

A 1950 home economics class at Little Rock Junior College. (UALR Archives Photo Collection 2, #39)

The annual Stunt Night — a high point of the college social year for over a quarter of a century. (1958 **Trojan)**

students trying to get to class. As early as 1950, student council president Bob Hall presented the case for a Coleman Creek bridge to the Little Rock School Board, the mayor of the city, and the Pulaski County Judge. City and county officials ignored Hall's efforts, and in the spring of 1955 the administration had to use the college truck to ferry pedestrians across the area flooded by Coleman Creek.[36]

In Jaycee's last years as a two-year institution the college maintained the friendly and personal atmosphere that had characterized it from the beginning. Each year the administration sponsored a parents' reception and expected every student "to bring at least one of his parents and see that he or she meets all of his instructors."[37] The administration encouraged married veterans to bring their wives to the function, which featured decorations and refreshments furnished by the college's home economics classes. Once LRJC expanded into a university with a student body of several thousand, activities like the parents' reception became impossible. Many supporters of the school maintained that by becoming too large for such events, the school lost a sense of community that had once been an important part of an LRJC education. Since LRJC remained a commuter school, and the student body was growing, that intimate atmosphere became increasingly difficult to maintain.

Part of the problem centered on the number of Jaycee students who had to work to underwrite the cost of their schooling. A 1954 campus survey estimated that approximately 67 percent of the LRJC students had some kind of employment outside their classroom work.

While most labored at traditional jobs like clerking or delivering papers, a few imaginative undergraduates earned their money working as tombstone engravers, or obituary writers, or musicians in the Arkansas Symphony. Other students achieved recognition for their writing skills. Lynn Babcock wrote a popular column in the *Arkansas Gazette* called "Young Little Rock" that dealt with the activities of the city's adolescent population; two LRJC poets — Barbara Wilmarth and Thomas Sperling — had their works selected to appear in the *National Anthology of College Poetry*.[38]

JC students also enjoyed a full range of social activities, many of which were annual campus events. Inaugurated in 1929, the semi-annual all-school picnic often attracted as many as 300 LRJC undergraduates. School officials originally held the picnic at Camp Pfeifer, but because of World War II restrictions they shifted the site to Boyle Park near the campus. The picnic featured competitions in softball, touch football, badminton, and bridge and offered the usual picnic fare of hot dogs, potato salad, and cold drinks.

For many years the Halloween Carnival attracted a large number of students. Held as a benefit for the athletic department, the Halloween festivities received enthusiastic support from the college's social clubs. In 1951, for example, the Battlecriers sponsored a kissing booth and held a variety show; the Zeta Phis ran a concession stand and a penny-pitching booth; the Phi Alpha fraternity sponsored a poker game; and the Sigma Taus held a dance in connection with the carnival.[39]

In the years following World War II, Stunt Night continued to be one of the most popular events on the Jaycee social calendar. One undergraduate in the early 1950s commented that "with each succeeding performance of Stunt Night the years have brought better arranged, better presented and more individualized acts, which give the student a feeling of growth and development along with the college."[40] Before Jaycee became a four-year school, Stunt Night drew crowds of over 800 people for student skits and musical presentations and provided the college loan fund with a reliable source of income each year.

Campus fraternities and sororities continued to provide additional activities for some students who desired a more active social life. Discriminatory in their selection of members, the fraternities and sororities on the LRJC campus never affiliated with national organizations. Each year the local clubs sponsored a host of hayrides, bingo parties, style shows, buffet suppers, and dances with numerous themes.

Between 1952 and 1955 the number of students participating in these and other campus functions declined as the overall enrollment at Little Rock Junior College temporarily dropped. As a result of the low birthrate in the early years of the Depression and the number of young men drafted into the Korean War, the ranks of college students decreased for a few years.

In 1951 LRJC had 457 daytime students and over 700 individuals in the night school program.[41] The ratio of men to women that had favored females during the war years had been completely reversed with 334 men and only 123 women students in the day classes. After a three-year decline the student body began to expand in the institution's last

years as a junior college. By September 1956 the enrollment reached 1,068, representing a 13.4 percent increase from the previous fall.[42] The growth of the student body after the early years of the decade indicated an increasing need for higher education in the central Arkansas area and fed the hopes of those who wanted to see George Donaghey's dream of a municipal university become a reality.

Hundreds of Little Rock Junior College alumni shared this dream. By the early 1950s LRJC graduates were beginning to have an impact on the development of the institution as well as the city of Little Rock. Organized in 1933, the college's Alumni Association annually awarded the G.J. Francis Memorial plaque — in memory of the first president of the campus YMCA, who died in an automobile accident — to an outstanding young man in each class, but otherwise the group went through several years of passivity in regard to the development of the college. Starting in 1947, however, the school's alumni had become involved in the Permanent Home Campaign and as a result approached the affairs of Jaycee with renewed enthusiasm. Also in 1947, Pauline Hoeltzel of the English department became the new alumni coordinator and circulated an alumni newsletter that stimulated new interest in the school. In 1950, 115 graduates contributed over $700 to a memorial fund for John Larson and began awarding the Shield of the Trojan plaque at commencement. The annual award signified that the recipient had "attained success in his field and had rendered great service to his alma mater."[43] The association gave the first Shield to Dr. Granville Davis, the recently appointed

president of the college, and subse-
quently honored an impressive group of
distinguished alumni in a similar fashion. (See the Appendix.) In 1942 one authority estimated that half of all the
teachers and administrators in the Little
Rock public school system either were
graduates of LRJC or had attended it,[44]
and by 1950 thirteen graduates of LRJC
held teaching or staff positions at their
alma mater, while other alumni assumed
leadership roles in the city's business
and professional community.

The growing strength of its alumni
paralleled the maturation of the college
itself. For many supporters of the institution the late 1940s and early 1950s
represented the height of its accomplishments as a two-year school. After set-
tling into life on the new Hayes Street
campus, many individuals connected
with LRJC began to see possibilities for
the school beyond the original vision of
John A. Larson. Those teachers and administrators recognized that for Jaycee to
develop, the academic accomplishments
of the college as well as the student life
at the institution had to rest on a solid
foundation.

*A member of the first graduating class at LRJC, Dr. Granville D. Davis — later an instructor of history and president of the college from 1950 until 1954. (1948 **Trojan)***

C H A P T E R S E V E N

Under New Leadership

*J*ust as student life and campus activities at Little Rock Junior College expanded in the early 1950s, the physical appearance of the school also improved. By 1952 city leaders had paved Hayes Street from the Hot Springs Highway to Markham Street, a step which, according to the Jaycee *Alumni News Letter,* gave many Little Rock citizens "their first real view of J.C."[1] Inside the campus, school officials paved all interior roads and built a new driveway west of the Chatter Grill that connected to the Hayes Street entrance, forming a complete drive through the college location. Surrounded by scenic pine trees and encircled by the new driveway, the modern classroom-library complex symbolized a new beginning for LRJC.

While a modern campus and an active student body formed essential elements in the "new" college, the administrative and academic life of LRJC also underwent substantial changes in the late 1940s and early 1950s. Following President Larson's death in November 1949, the college board appointed Dean Brothers as the school's acting president. Relying heavily on his department heads to conduct the daily business of the school, Brothers requested that his name not be considered for the full-time presidency.

"The college needs a young man for president," Brothers told a reporter from the campus paper. "One that can be here for a long time, not one that is close to retiring age."[2] The Little Rock School Board, acting as the board of trustees of the junior college, honored Brothers's wish and selected the new president from the teaching staff of the school. In May 1950, only five days before the end of the semester, it named LRJC history instructor Dr. Granville Davis as the institution's new president. Davis delivered a combination commencement address and inaugural speech at the graduation exercises at Robinson Auditorium on May 25, 1950.

Almost immediately the new president proved popular, intelligent, and competent. A heavy-set, jovial individual, Davis had been a member of Jaycee's first graduating class and had returned as an instructor in 1932, later receiving his Ph.D. degree from the University of Illinois. His "Arkansas and the Blood of Kansas" was the lead article in the November 1950 issue of the prestigious *Journal of Southern History,* and he contributed other articles to the *American Historical Review* and the *Arkansas Historical Quarterly.*

To improve the quality of education offered at LRJC, Davis visited junior colleges throughout the South and the Midwest, including Bradley Junior College in Peoria, Illinois; Joliet (Illinois) Junior College; and Asheville (North Carolina) Junior College. An outspoken supporter of strong academic programs for two-year schools, Davis criticized some of the institutions he visited for offering a trival, popularized curriculum that included classes in subjects like bridge. He reassured the LRJC community and the school's supporters in the capital city who had worked on the Permanent Home Campaign that throughout his journey "nowhere did I find a physical plant as modern and efficient as our own."[3] In November 1951 the citizens of Little Rock selected Davis Man of the Year, affirming their confidence that he was offering positive, effective leadership to make Little Rock Junior College one of the most outstanding two-year institutions in the region.

Part of the school's strength during this era came from a dedicated faculty. By the time Granville Davis assumed the office of president, a few early instructors like J.H. Atkinson, Pauline Hoeltzel, Elmer Stalhkopf, and Gladys Kunz Brown remained on the teaching staff, though many others had retired or moved to other institutions. Helen Hall, the first woman in the United States to receive a master of arts degree in journalism (also acclaimed for her children's book *My Dog Lucky)*, taught at both Jaycee and Little Rock Senior High School until 1943. John A. Bigbee, a popular mathematics instructor, died in 1947, and Blanche Martin became the first LRJC instructor to retire officially from teaching in 1948.[4]

Over the years the college replaced these instructors with an equally dis-

tinguished group of teachers including Cecil Edginton and Eleanor Orts in the English department, Orville W. Taylor in history, Dr. James H. Stevenson in biology, and James F. Fribourgh in zoology and chemistry.[5] In 1953 Dr. John P. Anderson moved from Hendrix College in Conway to become LRJC's first dean of students. In addition he taught sociology and psychology and a course in "Human Growth and Development" in the Jaycee adult education program.

By 1955 Little Rock Junior College had a faculty that included 26 full-time instructors and 8 part-time teachers. Two of the regular staff held doctorate degrees, 21 had earned master's degrees, and 3 had only a bachelor's degree. The average tenure of the Jaycee teaching staff exceeded nine and a half years, which according to one study indicated "a high degree of satisfaction and a high state of morale among the faculty."[6] A year later, the president of LRJC reported that the faculty salaries at the school compared favorably with other institutions in Arkansas, with a median nine-months' salary of $4,470. He also praised the faculty retirement system, and informed the board of trustees that he found "no major weaknesses in the faculty as to professional and community activities."[7]

Throughout the early 1950s the faculty actively shared in the planning and operation of the institution. The school's organizational structure called for seven standing committees that included all full-time members of the teaching staff. The committees dealt with areas affecting the life of the college like administration and finance, instruction, the library, the physical plant, personnel services, curriculum, health, and physical education and athletics. Moreover, a coordinating committee integrated the activities of the other standing committees, resulting in an efficient system of faculty involvement in the governing process of the college.[8]

In 1956 Jaycee instructors had a total of nineteen scholarly articles published in various journals, but they remained primarily a teaching faculty. Most maintained membership in the Arkansas Education Association; at least ten percent belonged to the National Education Association.[9] LRJC instructors also engaged in some professional activities. In November 1954 a group of Jaycee instructors formed a chapter of the American Association of University Professors and elected Orville Taylor as their first president.[10] Each year a delegation of LRJC instructors also attended the annual meetings of the National Conference on Higher Education. Full-time faculty members taught fifteen semester-hours each term, a load that compared favorably with those of junior college instructors throughout the country. Although often burdened with weekly attendance reports and other bureaucratic trappings, the Jaycee teachers received generally high marks from their own students. According to a mid-1950s survey, an overwhelming majority of LRJC undergraduates, when asked if they felt free to approach their teachers with personal as well as academic problems, answered in the affirmative.[11]

On the other hand, critics pointed out several problem areas in regard to the school's faculty. For example, the annual report of the president in 1956 indicated that only seven percent of the faculty held a doctorate, a figure the president felt needed to be increased to at least 35 percent.[12] An earlier study raised questions about the LRJC faculty's commitment to professional growth in terms of attending national and regional academic conferences and pursuing meaningful research in the individual instructor's chosen field.[13] Finally, despite comparisons with other Arkansas colleges, the Jaycee faculty remained poorly paid. A memorandum from acting president Brothers to the Little Rock School Board in May 1950 revealed that after 23 years of loyal service to the institution J.H. Atkinson and Pauline Hoeltzel still only earned $3,590 each per year.[14] Even with allowances for later inflated dollars, staff salaries at the school remained extremely low throughout the decade. This problem was compounded by the paltry pittance paid to part-time teachers. By 1950 most part-time instructors received only $66 a month for teaching a large three-hour class. This exploitive practice was to continue throughout the institution's later existence as Little Rock University and the University of Arkansas at Little Rock. Rather than hire a single full-time instructor, the administration often found the policy of engaging two or three part-time teachers less costly, and since the school rarely gave salary increases to part-time teachers the practice helped soften the blow of rising inflation.

Along with normal classroom duties, committees, and counseling work, many Jaycee faculty members helped recruit new students. Faculty recruitment had begun in 1934 under Atkinson's leadership, with the result that by 1939, according to him, "many students who would otherwise never have gone to college at all have secured the first two years here at Jaycee...."[15] By 1950 Atkinson coordinated a systematic program of visitation whereby a team of faculty members and administrators "called at the homes of all graduates of the four high schools of greater Little Rock."[16] School officials supplemented this effort with a "Campus Day" at the college when high school graduates could visit Jaycee, a mailing drive to inform younger pupils about the advantages of attending LRJC, and an advertising campaign in local and high school newspapers that stressed the college's accredition, the availability of student aid, and the fact that "the nearness of this institution to your home affords you advantages in securing the first 2 years of your college training with a minimum of expense."[17] Under Granville Davis's administration, Jaycee also dispatched faculty members to address high school assemblies and, on occasion, to show the film of the Trojans' victory in the 1949 Junior Rose Bowl game.[18]

Instructors at LRJC recognized that a successful junior college liberal arts program had to reflect the freshman-sophomore curriculum offered by most four-year institutions. In 1949 the revised Jaycee catalogue defined the curriculum as a series of courses "arranged as nearly as possible like those of the lower divisions in leading colleges and universities [as well as] two years of specialized education in the fields of business and the semi-professions...."[19] In the spring of 1949, President Larson appointed a faculty curriculum committee to recommend ways of improving the college's basic program. The committee acted as a clearinghouse for all proposed changes, reviewed potential new courses, and studied the possibility of someday expanding the existing LRJC

offerings into a four-year college.

In 1951, after an extensive survey of catalogues from other colleges, the committee successfully promoted the reorganization of the institution's courses into four divisions. The Humanities Division under Hoeltzel's chairmanship included courses in art, Bible, English, foreign languages, music, and speech; the Natural Sciences headed by Dr. James H. Stevenson offered courses in the biological sciences, physical sciences, and mathematics; the Social Sciences under Dr. Iva Cox Gardner featured programs in economics, history, political science, psychology, philosophy, and sociology; and the Division of Applied Arts and Sciences included courses in aeronautics, business administration, engineering, home economics, and physical education.

Underlying the efforts of the curriculum committee in the early 1950s was a belief in the necessity of keeping general education at the core of LRJC's program. Many Jaycee instructors feared that after World War II, too many colleges had started overspecializing and teaching not the "why" but rather the "what" of life. They wanted the college to avoid the pitfalls of technical education.[20] At a general faculty meeting in April 1950 Dean Brothers urged all Jaycee teachers to review the school's participation in the cooperative study in general education conducted a few years earlier, reminding the instructors that the objectives of general education included "to be able to think straight; be able to live with our fellow man; appreciate beauty and life and create beauty in life."[21] Over the years Jaycee had promoted general education and had allowed a certain amount of experimentation in the classroom. As early as 1940, Gladys Kunz Brown had allowed the students in her course on the contemporary novel to plan their own reading and set their own goals and objectives for the course. In 1948 the administration instigated an experimental program in remedial reading. In February 1954 President Davis proposed a total revision of the school's curriculum "to embrace a variety of courses of a general education nature [including] surveys of the humanities, the fine arts, social sciences, physical sciences and courses in Western Civilization and American Institutions … to give the student the most exciting educational experiences of his life."[22] Although Davis left Jaycee before he could implement the program, by 1957 as Little Rock Junior College began the process of becoming Little Rock University, the new president reported that the faculty had succeeded in preserving a system based on the concepts of Davis's proposal. "General education is the most characteristic feature of a superior institution," he said. "LRJC has an excellent program of general education. A major part of the curricula for the first two years at LRJC is general education and all of the courses for the freshman and sophomore years could be in general education if the student desired to elect them."[23]

In the early 1950s in many junior colleges throughout the United States, administrators abandoned the liberal arts and other traditional programs and instead began stressing vocational courses.[24] At LRJC, under Davis's leadership, the school tried to maintain the general education program in the day classes while emphasizing more practical courses in the evening division. In Janu-

ary 1951 Davis sent a letter to the school board regarding the night school, informing the trustees that "while general academic work has not been neglected, emphasis has been placed on practical courses which will be helpful to employers and employees in our business community."[25] As a result of this change, in the following years Jaycee night school courses in accounting, commercial law, marketing, salesmanship, air conditioning and refrigeration engineering, shorthand, and typing all reached record enrollments.[26] During the same period, several Little Rock business firms paid the tuition for their employees who enrolled in courses related to their jobs — a process that further linked the college and the community.

The LRJC administration accelerated this connection between the school and the city by promoting the idea of community service. During Davis's presidency the college sought to do more than train a local work force. Recognizing that 40 percent of Jaycee's graduates would not enter a senior college, but rather would seek employment in the greater Little Rock area, Davis wanted to train individuals for specific jobs that might be available when students completed their studies. For example, rather than limiting the training of secretaries to a general secretarial program, school officials sought to determine how many medical secretaries would be needed in the community and then establish a curriculum to produce graduates to fill those positions. In September 1951, in cooperation with the Baptist Hospital in Little Rock and Baylor University in Waco, Texas, Little Rock Junior College initiated a plan to train needed nurses. Under this system, students completed their freshman year at LRJC, trained at the Baptist Hospital, and then did a year of work at Baylor before receiving their nursing certificates.[27]

In addition to vocational education, LRJC inaugurated an extensive adult education program in the early years of the decade. Throughout the era, the college offered several non-credit courses in music appreciation, painting, creative writing, general science, and the Great Books program. More importantly, in 1951 the Ford Foundation selected Jaycee to participate in a three-year experiment in coordinated adult education. As the sponsoring agency for the program, the college, with Ford Foundation funding, employed a director to supervise adult education activities in the central Arkansas area. In the beginning the LRJC community demonstrated considerable enthusiasm for the project. In a letter to the school board, President Davis wrote that the citizens of Little Rock "would profit from the stimulation that such a program would afford and the college would benefit ... by enlarged enrollments and by an enlarged opportunity to serve the people of this area."[28] By 1953, under the supervision of director L.O. Baker, the school's experiment in "free liberal education for adults only" had an annual enrollment of over a thousand participants in tuition-free discussion classes in international relations, community problems, world masterpieces, and consumer economics.

Despite early enthusiasm, large enrollments, and worthwhile goals, LRJC's adult education program fell under severe criticism by the fall of 1954. In November of that year, Foster Vineyard wrote to Dean Brothers that "it would appear that for two or more years mon-

ey has been spent on the Adult Education Program without budgets being adopted or financial statements rendered periodically, or any control by the board of trustees over this activity."[29] The financial difficulties of the program became so great that the college applied to the Ford Foundation for a supplementary grant. In response to the school's request, John Osman of the foundation expressed concern over the state of the adult education program in Little Rock and told Vineyard that "at some time this program has to stand on its own. The present difficulty stems from the fact that only $1,800 was ever raised by LRJC as their part of the original matching grant that [sh]ould have been $12,000."[30]

Although in January 1955 LRJC officials dismissed the secretary of the Adult Education Program because of a lack of funds, they retained the director and completed the classes that had been scheduled for that spring. One disgusted board member commented that "last spring LRJC was at the top ... [N]ow they have to explain why Little Rock is a zero."[31] Because of a lack of local financial support and monetary mismanagement by the leadership of the program, the Jaycee administration discontinued the Ford Foundation Adult Education Program in the summer of 1955. After that date the junior college continued to offer educational opportunities to older students, but confined these efforts to the regular curriculum in both the day school and the night division.

To supplement that curriculum the administration expanded the John A. Larson Memorial Library during the school's last decade as a junior college.

In February 1946 Dean Brothers hired Mrs. L.H. Caldwell, a former missionary to China and friend of author Pearl Buck, as the college's new librarian. Mrs. Caldwell later remembered that "they first called on me to come to LRJC for two weeks, or until another librarian came. She never came, and my two weeks lasted into fourteen years."[32] Under Mrs. Caldwell's leadership the library grew to meet the needs of an increasing student body. In 1951 the facility acquired the L. Ernest Moore Manuscript Collection, which included thousands of original records of the federal occupation of Little Rock by General Frederick Steele during the Civil War; three years later Donald K. Hawthorne donated 1600 volumes to the general collection. In 1953 the John A. Larson Library received its own endowment in the form of a gift of Sterling store stock with the interest designated for the purchase of books. Moreover, in the early 1950s Mrs. Caldwell installed a new system of searching books and briefcases as students left the library. The librarian instituted the policy after conducting a survey showing a majority of colleges and high schools utilized the system. The institution maintained the searches after becoming a four-year school despite the complaints of a few who argued that the system cast doubt over the honesty of every student who used the library.

The book-check system did save the college money and consequently received the support of the administration even though the school's monetary situation remained relatively stable throughout the early part of the decade. The 1953-54 budget revealed that LRJC took in $143,000 in tuition, $75,000 from the Donaghey Foundation, and an additional $14,851 from miscellaneous donations for a total income of $232,851. Disbursements for the same year included $163,000 in salaries, $17,000 in maintenance, $28,000 in capital outlay, and $25,000 of miscellaneous spending for a total of $233,000.[33] A comprehensive survey conducted in 1955 indicated that the school's receipts had increased to $317,000 while operational expenses rose to only approximately $306,000. With a per-student cost of a low $373.52, the study found that on the eve of becoming a four-year institution, Little Rock Junior College "is financially in good shape."[34]

Because LRJC officials relied heavily on tuition for revenue to operate the institution, the availability of numerous scholarships not only enabled students from central Arkansas to attend the college, but also insured a steady source of income for Jaycee. One writer in the early 1950s observed that LRJC "in its role as a community college is the agency through which philanthropic individuals of Little Rock make scholarship grants to worthy young people."[35] In 1946 Fred W. Allsopp, a member of the Donaghey Foundation, left a $25,000 educational trust fund for the school at the time of his death, while a few years later A.W. Sloss bequeathed $10,000 to the board of trustees of Little Rock Junior College. Over the years Jaycee also received scholarship funding from Kathryn Neal as a memorial to her son, Dick Neal, an LRJC graduate; Mr. and Mrs. Q.L. Porter; Mrs. L.E. Moore; Mr. and Mrs. Graham Hall; John Pruniski, Senior and Junior; Mr. and Mrs. Leo Pfeifer; the Crow-Burlingame Company; the Lions Club of North Little Rock; the Grundfest Foundation; the Donaghey Foundation;

The Trojan basketball team battling the University of Arkansas freshmen in 1954. (1954 Trojan)

the Daughters of the American Revolution; the Parent-Teacher Association of Little Rock; the United Spanish War Veterans; and the Abigail Robinson Memorial. Most of the scholarships provided between $45 and $100 each semester, and although these aids were rather limited amounts by later standards, they nevertheless enabled a generation of Jaycee students to finance their education before assuming productive roles in the community.

The work of the college in educating these students became the focus of Little Rock Junior College's silver anniversary celebration in 1952. LRJC officials extended the festivities from May 1952 until May 1953 and used an anniversary theme in almost every event sponsored by the institution during that time. The school also held special exhibits of student and faculty artwork; presented a series of theatrical productions; and printed a colorful brochure which the administration mailed to alumni, members of the Little Rock Chamber of Commerce, and all graduates of local high schools.[36] The faculty and staff of the college used the anniversary to publicize Jaycee's achievements over the preceding 25 years and to call the attention of the people of central Arkansas to the future needs of the institution.

By the early 1950s Granville Davis and other leaders of LRJC recognized that in a matter of years the "war babies" — whose demographic enormity would move through American culture, as one historian later said, like a "pig through a python" — would be ready for college, and Jaycee would have to grow to meet the needs of hundreds of additional students. Before Little Rock Junior College would be ready to expand beyond the foundation built during the college's first quarter of a century, however, the school had to deal with a brief period of turmoil and crisis.

In many ways the collapse of the college's athletic program in the 1950s became the first sign Jaycee had entered an unstable era in the years before becoming a senior college. As early as 1947 a war veteran named Nick Vidnovic from Pittsburgh, Pennsylvania, had organized a varsity swimming team at Jaycee that won the state collegiate championship two years in a row, but after Vidnovic left the school, the administration let the swimming program languish. After the Junior Rose Bowl season of 1949, the school board selected W. Howard Pearce as the school's new athletic director and head football coach. A former player at both Arkansas Tech and the University of Arkansas, Pearce captained the southern team in the 1945 Blue-Gray all-star game in Montgomery, Alabama, and then became an assistant coach at Little Rock High School. Pearce's teams at LRJC played competitive football — the 1951 Trojans participated in the Lions Bowl game against Ellisville Junior College in Laurel, Mississippi — but none of the new coach's squads reached the heights of Jimmy Karam's 1949 team. In 1952 Pearce resigned and the trustees named Mervyn Greer as the school's new coach. After a 5-2-1 season, Greer also left. The administration selected Woody Johnson, a successful high school coach at El Dorado, to lead the Trojans, and in two seasons Johnson's teams posted a respectable 12-5-1 record.

Under all three coaches, various charitable groups used Little Rock Junior College football games as fund-raising

*The Trojans' Richard Nicolo in a game against Arkansas Tech in 1955. (1956 **Trojan**)*

events for their clubs. For example, in 1951 the Little Rock Junior League sponsored the "Speech Bowl" — a match between LRJC and Southern State College from Magnolia — and donated the proceeds of the game to the League's speech correction clinic. In 1953 the Pine Bluff Chamber of Commerce underwrote the Jaycee-Monticello A&M game and cleared over $500 for the organization.[37]

Also in the early 1950s, LRJC officials abandoned the school's membership in the Arkansas Intercollegiate Conference and briefly joined the Big Six, which included junior colleges from Tyler, Paris, and Kilgore, Texas, and similar schools from Cameron and Lawton, Oklahoma. President Davis of LRJC, in explaining the move, complimented the other Arkansas schools and expressed the opinion that football and basketball games between his institution and the colleges of the AIC "enabled us to reach understanding in many other areas besides athletics."[38] Davis also felt that since the schools at Magnolia and Monticello had become senior colleges, leaving LRJC as the only junior college in the conference, his institution had to join the Big Six. In the mid-1950s the last LRJC football teams, sparked by runningbacks Sam Richards and Richard Nicolo, defeated the University of Arkansas freshman team in War Memorial Stadium and posted an overall winning record in the school's new conference.

Despite these successes, school officials terminated intercollegiate football at Jaycee in December 1955. Throughout the first half of the decade, the Trojans had steadily been losing ground in terms of popular support to the emerging University of Arkansas program, placing the

LRJC administration in a quandary. As early as 1952, President Davis wrote to the director of athletics at Tyler Junior College in Texas that the day of the LRJC-Tyler football game "is also the date the U. of A. plays the University of Mississippi in an afternoon game here. It has been our experience in playing games the same day as the U. of A. results in a very poor gate. I am seeking your permission to play Friday evening instead of Saturday."[39] Playing Friday night games put the Trojans in competition with the local high schools, and attendance at the Jaycee games declined steadily. Furthermore, recruitment was hampered by the lack of athletic scholarships at LRJC,[40] and during the Korean War several key team members left school and joined the armed forces.[41]

Monetary factors also contributed to the demise of Jaycee football. The team often received a guarantee of only $200 or $300 to play a game away from Little Rock. Out of this amount Jaycee had to pay for lodging and food for the team, which usually left the school with a deficit to be made up with revenues from home games; but attendance in Little Rock declined because of competition from the Fayetteville program and the increasing popularity of football on television. Jaycee football became a losing proposition. School leaders tried to keep the team going by cutting expenses whenever possible and by selling used football equipment to struggling all-black colleges whose athletic programs were in worse shape than LRJC,[42] but on December 30, 1955, the college board voted to discontinue varsity football and instead established a new athletic policy stressing physical education classes and intramural competition.

The Field House, home of the Trojan basketball teams and of indoor intramural activities. (1952 ***Trojan)***

In the school's last decade as a two-year institution varsity basketball reappeared on the LRJC campus, but never equaled the early achievements of the football program. Part of the failure of the basketball Trojans resulted from the school board's reluctance to hire a qualified coach. In January 1947 the administration replaced Herman Bogan, a part-time coach and chemistry instructor, with George Haynie, the head track and assistant football coach at Little Rock High School. Haynie, who traveled to Jaycee from the high school each afternoon to supervise basketball practice, never gave the program adequate time, and the following year the board tapped Deno Nichols, a local radio announcer who had never coached before, to lead the Trojan roundballers.[43] Coaches then arrived and departed in rapid succession — John T. Floyd in 1950, James Bearden in 1951, John Kincannon in 1952, and head football coach Woody Johnson in 1953.

In 1952-53 the team played all Jaycee home basketball games in the high school gymnasium because the athletic department could not afford fold-away bleachers for the college's new field house. Also in the early fifties the Trojan basketball squad featured a player regarded by many observers as the best college player in the state at the time. Manuel Whitley from Bismarck averaged over 20 points a game for the Trojans before transferring to the University of Arkansas, where he later became a star. Despite Whitley's efforts, basketball, like football, declined at Jaycee and the administration finally abandoned basketball as a varsity sport in the middle of the decade.

To replace basketball and football, school officials relied on an intramural program under the direction of James W. Schultz, but the volleyball, basketball, softball, tennis, and golf competitions among the students never generated the enthusiasm of intercollegiate sports, and the absence of the Trojan teams tended to hurt student morale at the college. This situation intensified as the question of expanding Little Rock Junior College into a four-year institution became a major controversy at the school in the mid-1950s. As various factions debated the merits of the issue, the future of the college became uncertain and student morale declined further. Only after a long and sometimes bitter struggle over the creation of a senior college did a sense of optimism and enthusiasm return to the Hayes Street campus.

CHAPTER EIGHT

Toward a Municipal University

*I*n the years after his 1929 endowment gift, former governor George Donaghey often expressed his hope that some day "Junior" would grow up and reach maturity as a four-year collegiate institution. In his autobiography Donaghey posed the question, "Shall our plans and dreams lead to a four-year college with a fine new plant of its own?" The prospect of a senior college in the capital city, according to the ex-governor, "makes me feel stronger and younger."[1] Unfortunately, Donaghey died before Jaycee reached the status of a municipal university — a transition that generated one of the most bitter controversies in the history of Arkansas higher education. In many ways the conflict surrounding the creation of a four-year school reflected the broader struggle that took place in Little Rock in the 1950s between the forces that wanted to maintain the status quo of the pre-World War II era and those who wanted to propel the city forward into the modern world of the second half of the twentieth century.

By the middle of the decade the city of Little Rock had 110,000 people — over 200,000 when counted with North Little Rock and the surrounding areas. Since the end of the second world war, the city's population grew by eight percent while the state as a whole suffered a decline in the number of residents. Little Rock added at least a dozen major companies in the postwar era, including a large federal air base at nearby Jacksonville. Thousands of tract houses covered what had recently been the woodlands bordering the city. Suburban shopping centers, like the Village Shopping Center at Asher and Hayes Streets near the Jaycee campus that opened in 1957, started an exodus from the downtown area that altered the nature of the entire community.

By the mid-1950s, expansion and change became the hallmark of Little Rock's development; population and economic growth seemed to come easily. However, in some areas, notably race relations, the community did not accept change readily. Expanding higher education in the city lacked the drama and national headlines generated by racial integration, but nevertheless presented another example of part of the community's resistance to modernity.

The temptation to broaden into four-year institutions had plagued the junior college movement since its inception in the 1890s. Ambitious educators and community leaders always believed a full-fledged college had greater prestige and respectability than a local junior college, and over the years several quality two-year institutions unwisely expanded and became undistinguished four-year schools, subverting the mission of the junior college concept.

In Little Rock, dreams of extending LRJC into a four-year college dated back to the days when Jaycee held classes in the Little Rock Senior High School building. As early as 1932 John Larson spoke openly of enlarging his fledgling effort into a municipal university, telling audiences that, along with the need for a liberal arts school, "there is a real opportunity here for a college of business administration, as Little Rock is the business center ... of the state."[2] A decade later, the editor of the *College Chatter* observed that because of a letter written by Joe Woods, a Jaycee student, and published in the *Arkansas Gazette,* "the old question of making J.C. a four-year college has come to a boiling point."[3] In March 1941, school officials appointed a committee including G. DeMatt Henderson of the Donaghey Foundation board of trustees to discuss the possibility of LRJC's assuming senior college status. Because of the war in Europe and the chance of United States involvement, the committee delayed any decision on the matter.

After the war, the issue of expanding Jaycee became an important topic both at the college and in the community as a whole. The main impetus for broadening the school's program came from returning war veterans who sought to extend their education at Little Rock Junior College to include a bachelor's degree. One campus editor commented that the idea of a four-year college "is no longer an 'if' question. Just as the need for a junior college was realized and met

in 1927, so now, almost 20 years later, history repeats itself. Today there is a similar need for a senior college. The veterans want a senior college now. What could be a more fitting memorial to the former students who were killed in the war than a living memorial where young men and women perfect themselves as future leaders?"[4]

Between 1946 and 1949 a group of dedicated veterans including Wassell Burgess, Gene Sikes, Roger Howard, and Robert Diles promoted an effort to publicize the necessity of making LRJC a four-year school. In a series of radio programs, civic club speeches, and newspaper articles the GIs informed the public that without a bachelor's program in Little Rock they would have to seek admission to already overcrowded senior colleges throughout the state. A complete college would offer enormous economic benefits to the greater Little Rock area, they argued. The energy and sincerity of the veterans impressed their campus advisor, Granville Davis of the history department, and when Davis became president of the college in 1950 he initiated another drive to enlarge the college. In 1952, with the backing of the school board, Davis and the LRJC faculty conducted a thorough study of the school's potential to become a four-year college. The effort included a survey by Dr. Earl Anderson, a professor of education at Ohio State University, who met with the LRJC administration and staff in January 1953, October 1953, and February 1954, and suggested that Davis divide the faculty into committees to consider various phases of the program and facilities of the school and how they might be altered to meet the needs of a four-year institution. In his final report

Anderson wrote that in his judgment, "LRJC can be developed into a four-year college that can be approved by North Central as a four-year college within the next three or four years...."[5]

The Ohio State educator also recommended that the leadership of the school restrict the major areas of study to the humanities, the social sciences, the natural sciences, and business administration; increase the number of individuals holding the doctorate on the faculty; stimulate more active participation by the school's instructors in national and regional professional associations; and increase the amount of money spent on the library, as prerequisites to becoming a senior college.

While Anderson conducted his study, the college board also commissioned Dr. John Dale Russell, chancellor of the New Mexico Board of Education, to investigate the financial aspects of the transition of LRJC to a four-year school. Russell concluded the change could be accomplished easily and even indicated Jaycee could offer an additional two years of coursework with no increased funding from the Donaghey Foundation.[6]

In the meantime, President Davis acted on his own to hasten the process of creating a senior college in Little Rock. In August 1953 he wrote to Dr. John Tyler Caldwell, president of the University of Arkansas, suggesting that LRJC and the university combine to offer two courses in Little Rock at the junior level during the ensuing year. Davis informed his Fayetteville counterpart that LRJC needed to respond to numerous requests from war veterans in the capital city who had graduated from Jaycee and wanted to continue their schooling in Little Rock under the GI Bill. The Jaycee president also candidly told Caldwell that "we want to test the interest that students may have in taking junior-senior work with us."[7]

Caldwell responded positively to President Davis's overture. By September 1953 the two educators agreed to cooperate in offering two junior-level courses — "History of the West" and "Psychology of Normal and Abnormal Behavior" — during the fall term in Little Rock. Conducted through the Fayetteville campus's Division of General Extension, LRJC faculty members taught both courses. Caldwell and Davis also agreed that because of the experimental nature of the university-LRJC collaboration "neither institution would make a formal announcement concerning these courses but that knowledge of them would be spread by word of mouth through LRJC and the University Graduate Center."[8] In establishing the classes, the university president cautioned Davis that "no prospects" existed for any significant or long-range junior-senior cooperative work in Little Rock, although the Fayetteville administration supported the idea of a limited number of upper division courses in the capital city over the next few years.[9]

Davis followed up the agreement with Caldwell by hosting a meeting of the sophomore class at Little Rock Junior College to discuss the possibilities of the school's expansion and test student reaction to such a move.[10] The Jaycee students enthusiastically endorsed the proposed change. By late 1953 not only the undergraduates but the faculty and administration of LRJC as well as certain segments of the Little Rock community believed that the time had come for the college to become a four-year institution.

Acting on that sentiment, on May 12, 1954, the members of the Little Rock School Board, in their capacity as trustees for LRJC, passed a resolution recommending that the school "be expanded to a four-year, senior college, the third year to be added in September 1954, and the fourth year in September 1955."[11] The college board, which included Foster A. Vineyard, Mrs. Edgar F. Dixon, Dr. Edwin N. Barron, Mrs. Arthur E. McClean, R.A. Lile, and Dr. William G. Cooper, initiated the measure after considering the studies conducted by Anderson and Russell and moved on the issue in order to give the administration time to recruit needed new faculty members.

Despite all of the confidence and fervor expressed by the Jaycee community for creating a four-year college, on June 9, 1954, the prospects of enlarging Little Rock Junior College received a devastating blow when the Board of Trustees of the Donaghey Foundation adopted a resolution expressing grave doubts about the wisdom of the college board's decision. The Donaghey board went a step further and crippled any expansion program by stating that the trustees "are therefore not in a position at this time to obligate Foundation funds to J.C. for the ensuing year ...."[12]

The majority of the Donaghey board believed that making Jaycee a four-year school would be considerably more expensive than President Davis and the college board anticipated and the results would be an inferior senior college. "A good junior college," the trustees argued, "serving the need which such a college is designed to serve, is far preferable to a poor struggling senior

college, one which would struggle along for a few years and then fold just as they are doing every year all over the country."[13] Some board members also pointed out that the Donaghey Building and the Waldon Building had aged considerably since the establishment of the original trust in 1929. Since many physicians who constituted the major tenants of the buildings had started moving their practices to the western part of the city to be close to the major hospitals, the Donaghey board also foresaw a possibility that the foundation's revenue might be reduced and future expansion efforts might thus be undercut.

Before passing the resolution on June 9, the Donaghey Foundation trustees received reassurance from A.L. Barber, the attorney for the trust, that the board had broad powers and discretion and did not have to support the Little Rock School Board's decision in the matter.[14] Following the vote to deny funding to LRJC, on June 10, the college board invited the Donaghey Foundation trustees to a joint conference to discuss the question of making LRJC a senior college, but five days later a spokesman for the Donaghey trustees informed the college board that such a meeting would not be necessary since the foundation board had "taken final action on the matter."[15] Although the boards met together later that month, the members' inability to resolve their differences resulted in a crisis over the future of Little Rock Junior College.

Part of the ensuing controversy stemmed from ill-defined areas of authority by the three boards that governed the affairs of the junior college. Since John Larson founded the institution in 1927, the Little Rock School

Board, functioning under the name of the Board of Trustees of Little Rock Junior College or simply the college board, had made policy for the school that had been carried out under rules and regulations established by campus authorities. Following the creation of the Donaghey Trust, the Donaghey Foundation directors managed the properties deeded in the trust and conveyed the resulting funds to the college. According to long-time school superintendent R.C. Hall, the Donaghey trustees, however, had "no hand in directing college affairs."[16] During the first decade of the operation of the trust, because of large interest payments on the mortgage on the properties, the Donaghey Foundation only gave the college a total of $9,340, and the trustees left the operation of the college to the school board. After 1938 and the refinancing of the mortgage payments, the contributions to the college became larger, and after 1948 when the annual income of $9000 to Mrs. Donaghey ceased at her death, the foundation's contribution to the school increased dramatically. With the retirement of the mortgage in 1950 the distribution to the college exceeded $45,000 and by 1953 the foundation donated $75,000 to Little Rock Junior College each year.[17] Because of the greater financial responsibility for Jaycee, several trustees of the foundation felt the Donaghey board needed to take a more active role in the direction of the college's development and consequently felt obligated to stop the disbursement of funds when President Davis and the college board took steps to expand LRJC to a senior college.

The lines of authority became further blurred with the establishment of the Little Rock Junior College Foundation in 1948. Created for the Permanent Home Campaign, the LRJC Foundation owned the land donated to the college by Raymond Rebsamen, held the title to all of the campus buildings, and conducted all of the college's major fund-raising campaigns. In 1952 when the Donaghey Board refused a plea by President Davis for additional funds, he submitted an identical request to the Little Rock Junior College Foundation — an act that generated some animosity on the part of some of the Donaghey trustees toward him.[18]

By 1954 and the controversy over the expansion of the school, President Davis found himself trapped in a struggle for authority between the directors of the Donaghey Foundation and the members of the Little Rock School Board. The leadership of the Little Rock Junior College Foundation assumed a low profile during the conflict, which left the future of the college in doubt pending the outcome of the battle between the other two boards.

Throughout the summer of 1954, the remaining two governing bodies clashed on several fronts, resulting in a confused situation that left LRJC with no president for a while and little hope of ever becoming a four-year institution. On July 1, the college board rescinded the resolution to expand in order to recover the $75,000 annual appropriation from the Donaghey Foundation. Foster Vineyard issued a public statement that "without that money Jaycee would be out of business by fall. Rather than see that happen we agreed to drop our plan."[19] The next day Charles L. Thompson, chairman of the Donaghey Foundation board, confirmed that "the understanding [was] that if the four-year plan was dropped we would give the college the money for next year."[20] On July 6 the Donaghey trustees unanimously voted to grant LRJC's request for $75,000 for the ensuing year for the "present Junior College."

The public response to the trustees' efforts to kill the expansion plan generally criticized the board for lacking a progressive outlook. In a series of editorials the *Arkansas Gazette* contended that the central issue in the whole affair involved which board had control of Little Rock Junior College. If the college board could be overruled by the Donaghey trustees on the question of enlargement, the *Gazette* writer argued, the Donaghey Board in effect ran the college.

Several critics raised the question of why the state's largest city should be served by only a two-year school while ten smaller communities in Arkansas had four-year institutions. One writer commented that "the very fact it [LRJC] has been a junior college since its founding in 1927 is scarcely an indication of Little Rock's progressiveness."[21] Woody Johnson, the LRJC football coach, told reporters that the decision not to expand had dealt a major blow to the school's athletic program, which had been geared to the addition of a third year for the fall term. The alumni association held a protest meeting in the auditorium of the Union Life Insurance building "to keep alive plans for the enlargement of the college to four years."[22] The alumni passed a resolution deploring the events of the summer which blocked the "opportunity for advanced formal education for the citizens of Little Rock and the surrounding community," and Roger H. Howard, the president of the alumni organization, wrote to Charles L. Thompson of the Donaghey board urging the

trustees to reconsider their efforts to block the extension of LRJC. Contending that since central Arkansas had become the largest population center in the state, resulting in an urgent need for advanced college courses, Howard asked Thompson to consider allowing Jaycee to become a local college without dormitories or the trappings of a statewide institution.[23] Even the students at Jaycee became involved in the controversy. One undergraduate wrote to Leo Pfeifer of the Donaghey board informing him that "the disappointment was general throughout the evening student body, as we learned of the trustees' postponement to start a four-year or a three-year school."[24]

Community sentiment to the contrary, the Donaghey Foundation board members maintained their position that Jaycee could not afford to expand to a senior college. Speaking for the trustees, Charles L. Thompson stated that "we are not interested in a four-year college. We're interested in a junior college. Would you want to ruin the junior college? That's the position we're in. They [the college board] would ruin the junior college."[25] The only dissent from this position came from William Nash, the single attorney on the Donaghey board, and Leo Pfeifer, who said that when Governor Donaghey asked him to serve on the board they both expressed a wish that the school would someday become a four-year institution. On several occasions Nash questioned not only the propriety of the trustees' intervention in the matter, but also the basis of their objections to the creation of a senior college, arguing that the original deed in trust clearly gave the foundation the power to contribute to a four-year school.

The controversy continued when the college board invited the Donaghey trustees to join in a friendly lawsuit to define the authority of the two boards. Initially the Donaghey board refused the offer and suggested a joint meeting could resolve any major differences.

Before any agreement could be reached, however, Granville Davis resigned as president of Little Rock Junior College. Citing the continued friction between the two boards over authority to determine policy for the college, he issued a resignation statement informing the supporters of the college that "I found myself in an impossible situation ... told by the school board to expand only to have that policy vetoed by the Donaghey Foundation without granting a hearing to the college board or the president of the college."[26] Davis also indicated that even though LRJC had earned the reputation of being a quality two-year institution, over the preceding months students, faculty, and scholarship donors had all expressed a lack of confidence in the ability of the two boards to run the affairs of the college. According to the school's president, "the damage done will be hard to repair ... The Big Question is the authority of the two boards. Here is a peril that can break the back of the college."[27] He blamed the Donaghey board for imperiling the institution and felt that the foundation trustees had created a hopeless situation that would not allow LRJC to grow and develop. Long after the controversy had died, Davis's successor told one interviewer that "the Donaghey Board pushed Granville Davis out."[28]

Although the college board appointed Dean Brothers to serve as acting presi-

dent of the college, the morale of the Jaycee community continued to decline. Vineyard indicated that the controversy during the summer might affect the college's accreditation. Many supporters felt LRJC had lost a valuable asset in the leadership of Granville Davis. Several faculty members expressed the opinion that Davis had been an excellent president during his tenure at the school, and one Jaycee graduate wrote an open letter to the *Arkansas Gazette* saying, "Dr. Davis is an outstanding educator .... He has a flexible, aggressive, and creative mind. It is seldom that educators of his stature remain in the South."[29] Davis did choose to remain in the region after leaving the presidency of Little Rock Junior College; in the fall of 1954 he became the executive director of the Ford Foundation-sponsored Memphis Adult Education Center.

Following Davis's departure, the members of the college board continued their fight to make Jaycee a senior college. Five days after the president resigned, the board filed a petition in the chancery court of Pulaski County seeking a declaratory judgment defining the proper authority of each of the college's governing bodies. At a meeting on August 12, 1954, the board, assured of the $75,000 allocation from the Donaghey Foundation for the 1954-55 school year, voted to rename Little Rock Junior College "Donaghey College" effective July 1, 1955, and passed a resolution stating that not later than that date "the college declare itself as moving toward a four year institution."[30]

When the case of *Little Rock Junior College vs. the George W. Donaghey Foundation* came to trial before the chancellor on October 4, 1954, attorneys for the

Gus Ottenheimer, chairman of the citizens' task force that paved the way for expansion to LRU in 1955, and longtime member of the board of trustees.

Donaghey trustees tried to prove that when a junior college converted to a senior college, the junior college ceased to exist and in such circumstances the senior college became a separate institution rather than a successor of the two-year school. Moreover, the lawyers sought to establish that the overwhelming expenses involved in changing a junior to a senior college in terms of new faculty, laboratory equipment, and library facilities would financially ruin the college in Little Rock. The college board, on the other hand, tried to prove that only the Little Rock School Board had the power to make policy for LRJC and that by threatening to deny needed funds to the school, the trustees of the Donaghey Foundation had usurped that authority.

After hearing testimony from both sides, Pulaski County Chancellor Rodney Parham ruled that the Donaghey Foundation could legally withhold all financial support from Little Rock Junior College if the college board proceeded with plans to convert the institution into a four-year school. Parham's judgment stunned the supporters of expansion. Vineyard, in something of an understatement, said the ruling put the Little Rock School Board in a "tough position."[31]

Attorneys for the college board appealed the verdict, and on March 28, 1955, the Arkansas Supreme Court in a 4-to-3 decision reversed the ruling of the Pulaski Chancery Court, declaring that the trustees of the Donaghey Foundation could not arbitrarily deny the college the profits of the trust. This decision effectively removed the major obstacle hindering the conversion of LRJC to a four-year institution.

In order to facilitate this change, the trustees of the Donaghey Foundation and the members of the college board held a joint meeting on May 14, 1955. The membership of the two boards decided not to select a new president for LRJC until an agreement had been reached on the future of the institution and voted to maintain the college for at least another year as a two-year school. To bring about an orderly resolution of the school's difficulties, the governing boards created a citizens' task force to study the situation and make recommendations as to whether or not the leadership of the college should create a senior institution from the foundation of Little Rock Junior College. The members of the school board also agreed to defer changing the school's name to Donaghey College until the task force had an opportunity to present its recommendations.

At the May 14 meeting, the joint boards appointed Gus Ottenheimer, a retired Little Rock industrialist, to head the citizens' committee. A civic leader and a fourth generation Little Rockian, Ottenheimer had graduated from Washington and Lee University in Virginia before returning to Little Rock in 1925 and joining his brother Leonard in establishing Ottenheimer Brothers, a ladies' ready-to-wear manufacturing company on East Markham Street. In 1955 the Ottenheimer brothers sold their business to the Sears corporation and Gus Ottenheimer assumed the chairmanship of the LRJC citizens' task force.

Although Ottenheimer had no previous connection with the institution, his involvement in 1955 became so extensive that the task force gained recognition as the "Ottenheimer Committee." He later

*The snack bar, 1956. (1956 **Trojan**, 45)*

served a twelve-year term on the school's board of directors and, following a merger with the University of Arkansas, became a member of the reorganized institution's Board of Visitors. For the 1955 committee, Ottenheimer recruited a group of distinguished citizens including Reverend R.D. Adams; Stonewall J. Beauchamp; Mrs. Noland Blass; G. Ted Cameron; August Engel; Dave Grundfest; Frank Lyon; Frank Newell; Hugh Patterson; Beloit Taylor; and Wallace Townsend to act as the executive committee of the 42-member task force to study the prospects for the future of the college.[32] The Donaghey Foundation paid the committee's expenses.

The group promptly hired three professional educators to conduct an initial survey of the educational situation in the capital city. Starting in August 1955 Dr. E.A. Lichty, a professor of education at Illinois State Normal School, Dr. W.W. Carpenter, a professor of education at the University of Missouri, and Dr. W.W. Reynolds, an educator from the University of Texas, studied various facets of LRJC and the educational needs of the surrounding community and submitted a series of recommendations to the Ottenheimer Committee. Upon the completion of the professional survey, Ottenheimer divided his group into subcommittees to investigate the situation further and to aid the executive committee in drafting its final report. In addition, the Ottenheimer Committee surveyed community sentiment toward Little Rock Junior College and researched the city's industrial and cultural potential as well as population trends in central Arkansas. Finally, before offering advice, members of the committee

interviewed representatives of the University of Arkansas, spokesmen from the Little Rock Chamber of Commerce, LRJC students, and alumni of the college, and studied a detailed report from the Jaycee faculty on the college's physical facilities, library, governance structure, faculty, curriculum, student life, and finances.[33]

Although some committee members disagreed over the community's ability to finance a senior college, the group expressed a unanimous opinion that the city of Little Rock needed a four-year collegiate program.[34] Because the majority of the membership of the Ottenheimer Committee came from the city's business sector, they emphasized that out of 29 southern cities "with which Greater Little Rock is competing in obtaining new industries ... 26 have one or more senior colleges. Little Rock therefore stands out conspicuously as lacking in higher educational opportunities."[35]

When the Ottenheimer Committee submitted its final recommendations to the Little Rock School Board and the Donaghey Foundation board of trustees in May 1956, the document focused on the overwhelming sentiment in central Arkansas for the establishment of a four-year college. The report showed that most LRJC students came from middle- or higher-income families, and a majority planned to continue their education beyond the junior college level. The committee also presented some of the same arguments that had been used almost 30 years earlier in creating a two-year school in Little Rock. Pointing out that the availability of jobs in the metropolitan area enabled numerous students to work their way through school, it contended that a senior college in the capital city "would afford a higher education to many of our students who otherwise would not be able to obtain one."[36] Finally, the committee's educational survey revealed that more than 50 percent of the graduates of Central High School in Little Rock attended college while in North Little Rock approximately 35 percent pursued higher education. Using these figures, the group projected that, with the anticipated rise in student-aged population in the area, the potential for increased enrollment in a local senior college was enormous.

The report praised the accomplishments of Little Rock Junior College over the school's 28 years of existence, complimenting the faculty and the administration for developing a quality two-year liberal arts program. However, the Ottenheimer Committee chastised the school's leadership for not doing enough to provide a self-contained curriculum for students who wanted only two years of technical training. The committee consequently recommended that even if the governing boards created a senior college, they should maintain a two-year program of vocational courses in technical and semi-professional fields.[37]

Specifically, the Ottenheimer Committee sanctioned the idea that Little Rock Junior College should be expanded to a four-year institution by 1961 and suggested that when the college reached senior status the governing body change the name of the school to the "George W. Donaghey College of Little Rock."[38] It further prescribed that the new school enter into an agreement with the University of Arkansas by which the Fayetteville school would conduct the junior and senior years of college work in Little

Rock. "My concept," Ottenheimer said in 1956, "is that the college would furnish the buildings and most of the facilities. The University would furnish the staff for the upper two years. I think the University would be interested in coming into the Little Rock area to serve the needs of an area which has about 10 percent of the state's population."[39] The industrialist tried to alleviate anticipated concerns that such an arrangement would in some unforeseen way interfere with the Razorback football team, by pointing out that the new system would simply enhance the educational opportunities for the undergraduates in central Arkansas who could not afford to go away to school in Fayetteville and would in no way compete with the university in other areas. As outlined in the committee report, under the proposed structure graduating seniors would receive diplomas from the University of Arkansas which would "carry a higher recognition for many years to come than that of a new and relatively unknown four-year college."[40] Moreover, the committee hoped that the existing junior college would remain intact to continue conducting freshman and sophomore classes and granting junior college certificates and degrees.

In an almost prophetic paragraph, the Ottenheimer Committee recommended that the election of a president for the Little Rock school should be done after consultation with the president of the University of Arkansas "in order that a man with proper temperament and personality ... can be selected who will eliminate the possibility of conflicting authority between the two segments of the college."[41] In fact, this conflict did arise several years later, but immediately after the release of the Ottenheimer report President Caldwell of the University of Arkansas stressed that no commitment to the institution in Little Rock had been made by the Fayetteville school and none would be forthcoming until further study had been undertaken.

Recognizing that an arrangement between the Fayetteville and Little Rock campuses might prove impossible, the Ottenheimer Committee further recommended that even without support from Fayetteville, LRJC should expand to a senior college financed by either increased tuition or a community-raised endowment fund, or, if possible, by amending the state constitution to allow citizens in the three Pulaski County school districts to vote for a millage tax to support the school. Regardless of the source of revenue, the committee believed any senior college in Little Rock should remain essentially a commuter or non-dormitory school.[42] Again and again, the report stressed that Little Rock needed a college for students who lived in the surrounding area and that therefore Jaycee officials should not even consider the question of campus housing.

In addition to the expansion of LRJC and the proposed arrangement with the University of Arkansas, the Ottenheimer Committee also sanctioned the creation of an autonomous governing board of trustees for the school apart from the Little Rock School Board. Under the direction of the new board, the committee hoped the school would quickly raise sufficient funds to finance the construction of a student union building, a science building, and a machine shop along with general grounds improvements. They also suggested that the Donaghey trustees increase the foundation's annual allocation to the college from $75,000 to $90,000.

The presentation of the Ottenheimer report in May 1956 proved to be a major turning point in the history of Little Rock Junior College. The very existence of the Ottenheimer Committee represented joint action by the college board and the Donaghey trustees, despite the Arkansas Supreme Court's having ruled the year before that the LRJC board had sole and complete authority to direct the school's destiny. Following the distribution of the committee's recommendations, the Donaghey Foundation trustees changed their earlier position and issued a statement pledging "wholehearted cooperation" with any effort to expand LRJC to a four-year school. The trustees also agreed to follow the Ottenheimer Committee's suggestion and increase the foundation's annual contribution to Jaycee to $90,000, promising that "the Foundation will do its utmost to make the senior college a great success."[43] Recognizing the overwhelming community sentiment that favored creating a four-year school in Little Rock, they quietly ended the controversy that had threatened the future of Little Rock Junior College, thus paving the way for the establishment of a new institution of higher learning in central Arkansas.

On August 16, 1956, the college board met at the Albert Pike Hotel and unanimously elected Dr. Carey V. Stabler as the new president of LRJC at an annual salary of $12,000. A former dean at both Shepherd College at Shepherdtown, West Virginia, and Florence State College at Florence, Alabama, the 49-year-old Stabler had received his bachelor's and master's degrees from the

*President Carey V. Stabler, who guided the institution through the LRU years. (1964 **Trojan**)*

University of Alabama and his Ph.D. from Duke University.[44] Charged with the task of overseeing LRJC's transition to a senior college, the new president later recalled that Lee Rogers, a Little Rock sporting goods dealer who had been a student of Stabler's at the University of Alabama, first recommended his name to the college board. Stabler also said that he wanted to come to Little Rock because he liked the potential for a private institution like LRJC to develop into a thriving city college.[45]

The new president assumed his duties on September 1, 1956. Stating that the college would soon become a four-year school without the aid of the University of Arkansas because of Fayetteville officials' reluctance, Stabler indicated that a capital fund drive to raise money for new buildings on the campus would begin soon and, he hoped, that faculty salaries could soon be raised as well. At that juncture the future of the institution rested with the citizens of the metropolitan Little Rock area — whose positive response over the next few years insured that the community would have increased educational opportunities for generations to come.

C H A P T E R   N I N E

Whatever Happened to Donaghey College?

*I*n October 1955, the members of Little Rock Junior College's Student Government Association voted to cancel the school's annual Halloween carnival. In the past the event had been a successful fund-raiser for the Jaycee athletic program, but with the administration's deemphasis on varsity athletics the carnival had dropped in popularity, netting only $2.50 in 1954. The abandonment of the carnival had broader implications, symbolizing a general decline of morale at the institution. Uncertainty about the school's future status, the resignation of popular president Granville Davis, and the absence of the Trojan football team all contributed to a sense of apathy on the campus that one student called "a disintegrating force such as must have been felt dimly by the leaders of Rome just before the empire fell."[1] Despite the best intentions of a faculty committee on student life[2] and an effort by the board of trustees to finance additional social functions at the college,[3] the atmosphere at Jaycee remained gloomy throughout the middle of the decade.

Part of the college's malaise resulted from a lack of recognition by the local community. The report of the Ottenheimer Committee called attention to LRJC's need for a program of public relations and referred to the absence of an effort to inform the public of the school's activities as "perhaps the weakest part of the J.C. program."[4] As early as 1944, the administration appointed Elizabeth Harden, an English and speech instructor, as the institution's official publicity director, and in 1949 Jaycee acquired the services of J. V. Dabbs, a former public relations executive with the Boy Scouts of America, but their combined efforts failed to overcome the college's obscure position in the Little Rock community.

Both the decline in student morale and the lack of recognition by the public began to change in 1957 when Little Rock Junior College underwent a dramatic transformation and became Little Rock University. A month after assuming his new office in August 1956, President Carey V. Stabler urged the college board to add a third year to the school "as soon as financial support and other circumstances will permit."[5] That same month the administration formed nine faculty committees to conduct a self-study of LRJC to serve as a foundation for expansion to a senior college; on March 15, 1957, the board voted 4-to-2 to add a junior year to the college in September.[6] Two months later the board reached the final decision to make Jaycee

*An outward sign of the change from Little Rock Junior College to Little Rock University in 1957. (1960 **Trojan,** 6)*

a complete senior college by adding a fourth year beginning in September 1958. Based on the recommendations of the faculty, the trustees approved a structure for the new school that consisted of four schools offering three degrees — the Bachelor of Arts degree from the School of Arts and Sciences; the Bachelor of Science degree from the Schools of Business and Education; and two-year degrees and certificates from the junior college.

Throughout the summer and early fall of 1957, President Stabler worked with the school's deans, division chairmen, and faculty to organize new courses, list degree requirements, and establish a program that would eventually meet the accreditation requirements of the North Central Association of Colleges and Secondary Schools. The administration also hired six additional faculty members and began planning for the further expansion of the Hayes Street campus.

When classes began in September 1957, two specific changes symbolized the inauguration of a new era in the school's history. The most obvious was a new name — Little Rock University. Although both the members of the college board and the Ottenheimer Committee favored calling the school "Donaghey College" in honor of the institution's largest benefactor, President Stabler soon after his arrival from Alabama launched a quiet campaign for another appellation that would carry broader implications. Since the local Catholic diocese had once operated an institution called Little Rock College, Bishop Albert L. Fletcher legally cleared the name so the new senior college could become "Little Rock College,"[7] but

Stabler pressed for an even more impressive designation. After researching the matter with officials of the North Central Association, Stabler learned that the accreditation criteria for an institution bearing the title "university" would be the same as that for one designated a "college." As a result, in February 1957 the Little Rock school's president told several trustees that at the next board meeting he planned to suggest naming the institution the "University of Little Rock."[8]

By May 22, 1957, Stabler had changed his mind and asked the board to consider the name "Little Rock University." Arguing that a city the size of the Arkansas capital would soon need a university and maintaining that calling the school a "college" would restrict the institution's development, Stabler urged the board to think in the broadest possible terms and rename Jaycee "Little Rock University." College trustees readily accepted Stabler's idea and voted that effective June 1, 1957, the institution would officially become Little Rock University.[9]

The institution would not be the first to have that name; in 1882, the Freedmen's Aid Society of the Northern Methodist Church had operated a Little Rock University on the east side of Main Street between Fourth and Fifth Streets. Although school officials moved the original LRU to a site on Lincoln Avenue overlooking the Arkansas River in 1883, the college closed in 1889 because of financial difficulties and a lack of public support.[10]

Along with a new name, the absences of history instructor J.H. Atkinson and Dean E.Q. Brothers when classes began in September 1957 evidenced a turning point in the school's development. Both men had retired during the summer of 1957 and received engraved wrist-watches at a dinner in their honor at the Sam Peck Hotel. One of LRJC's original faculty members, Atkinson had not only taught classes but also served on numerous committees, sponsored student organizations, helped undergraduates acquire financial assistance, and recruited new students for the school. In his 30 years of service to Little Rock Junior College, Atkinson came to personify the hardworking, dedicated junior college instructor. Brothers, after 27 years at LRJC as dean and, on two occasions, acting president, took emeritus status in 1957 and became manager of the campus bookstore. Both Atkinson and Brothers had played key roles in the college's growth for over a quarter of a century, and their absence symbolized the end of the school's embryonic years as a junior college.

Two years after the inauguration of this new era, 28 seniors received diplomas at the first commencement exercises at Little Rock University. The graduating seniors wore black robes with white collars to distinguish them from the blue-clad sophomores receiving junior college certificates. Dr. Harvie Branscomb, chancellor of Vanderbilt University in Nashville, Tennessee, delivered the commencement address. To the many individuals who had helped transform Little Rock Junior College into Little Rock University, the graduation ceremony seemed to validate their efforts and to mark the beginning of the institution's history as a private senior college.

During the early years of that period, Little Rock University moved to a new level of financing the college's programs.

In October 1956 the college board officially approved a major capital funds drive under the auspices of the Little Rock Junior College Foundation (the organization that later became the Little Rock University Foundation, Inc.). Completed in March 1957, the campaign raised almost $650,000 to finance the transition from a junior college to a four-year school, build a modern science building, and make major campus improvements. Under the chairmanship of Little Rock businessmen Robert D. Lowry and Chris Finkbeiner, the foundation conducted an intense publicity campaign and fund-raising drive under the slogan "Little Rock needs a four-year college now!"

The literature and rhetoric surrounding the drive emphasized that a senior college would help attract new business and industry to central Arkansas as well as providing the young people of the area with the opportunity to acquire a college degree without having to leave home.[11] One letter from the foundation's executive committee to the campaign workers even told the volunteers that "unless you 'sell' the LRJC expansion program, you may deny some worthy boy or girl the opportunity of an education that he or she could not obtain otherwise."[12]

The drive generated enthusiastic support from the college community. The faculty contributed more than $8000 and undergraduates over $5000. The administration excused students from classes to solicit money, and one day over 300 students marched down Main Street in the rain in an effort to publicize the school's need for funds.[13] Despite these efforts, and substantial contributions from corporations like the Arkansas

Power and Light Company, the capital funds campaign made slow progress. In January 1957 John H. Rule of the Donaghey Foundation wrote to chairman Robert D. Lowry expressing his concern. "We [the Donaghey Foundation trustees]," he wrote, "are very much disturbed by the apparent reluctance so far of a large segment of the community to measure up to its financial responsibility in connection with the present campaign. It just must not fail."[14]

Contributions increased toward the end of the drive and, by raising $650,000, the campaign certainly did not fail. President Stabler expressed satisfaction with the results at the time and confided to a later interviewer that "I wouldn't say [the capital funds drive] was a real disappointment to me because we had set the goal [$850,000] higher than we actually had to have so what we got was sufficient for going ahead ...."[15]

To enhance LRU's financial position further, the board of trustees also raised the school's tuition from $140 per semester to $192 per semester for a full class load of sixteen hours, increasing the per-semester-hour fee from $11 to $12. In addition, beginning in the fall of 1957, the administration charged a building fee of $30 per year for full-time students with proportionate amounts billed to part-time students.[16] In 1958, Stabler made a fact-finding tour of several municipal colleges, including the University of Omaha, the University of Kansas City, Oklahoma City University, and Tulsa University and reported to the college board in Little Rock that, while LRU's tuition remained at $12 an hour, the other institutions averaged $20 per semester-hour. The board, however, decided not to increase tuition at the new senior college until 1962 when the members of the board raised the tuition to $15 a semester-hour.

Partly to offset low tuition rates, Little Rock University did have access to additional funds. By the late 1950s, the Donaghey Foundation provided the college with an annual distribution of $90,000 along with smaller grants for specific purposes. With the conclusion of the lawsuit in 1955, the Donaghey trustees remained committed to the success of the new four-year school. In January 1960 the president of the foundation responded to an inquiry from a college president in Michigan informing him that "it is utterly remote, in fact, impossible, that at any time in the future the trustees of the Donaghey Foundation would want to transfer the beneficence away from Little Rock University."[17]

To supplement the revenues from tuition and the Donaghey Foundation, the school's alumni association instituted an annual fund-raising drive in 1961. Under the direction of alumni president John Blundell, the first campaign generated $500 and the second one over $1500. Awareness of the college's need for money led the board of trustees in 1962 to create the "110," an effort to get 110 members to contribute $25 a year to the alumni fund for campus projects like the library, the band, and a memorial portrait of Dean Brothers, who died in 1959.

President Stabler also played a role in fund-raising. In the early years of the school's development, revenue from tuition and the Donaghey Foundation had proven sufficient to maintain the institution. By the early 1960s, however, the duties of a college president had expanded to include raising money to

*Business manager Francis Robinson discussing campus expansion with the driver of a bulldozer. (1961 **Trojan**)*

meet the needs of a growing student body and an expanding academic program. Toward that end, in late 1962 Stabler attended the President's Seminar on Fund Raising in Detroit, Michigan. Subsidized by the Ford Motor Company, the series of meetings drew over 50 college and university presidents who studied development systems, fund-raising techniques, and methods of securing federal aid for their respective institutions. With this type of training, the president of Little Rock University demonstrated a capacity to raise a modest amount of additional funding for the college each year. Although the school received few enormous single gifts during Stabler's sixteen-year tenure, LRU did obtain numerous donations and grants from both corporate and private donors.

This growth of revenue for the university between 1957 and 1963 enhanced the role of the school's business manager, a post the administration filled in 1956 by hiring Francis L. Robinson. A former secondary school teacher and principal of Quitman High School, Robinson played a leading part in the expansion of the campus and the development of the LRU staff. In an interview conducted 30 years later, on the eve of his retirement as vice-chancellor for finance of the University of Arkansas at Little Rock, Robinson recalled that "the job I had grew much larger. Instead of just being a business manager, I had responsibility for physical plant, financial affairs, security, purchasing, planning, student aid and scholarships, and construction projects."[18] Under Robinson's leadership the school implemented a series of modern business practices designed to promote efficiency and service[19] and began to develop an excel-

lent support staff. In 1960 Robinson's office, under the direction of the Finance Committee of the board of trustees, initiated a program of depositing the school's funds in local banks on a rotation basis — a practice that maintained good will for the college throughout the entire Little Rock financial community.[20]

By 1960, because of increased tuition, the support of the Donaghey Foundation, and various gifts, the examining team from the North Central Association found that LRU had "financial resources more than adequate to meet minimum standards for an institution of its size and type."[21] While in 1955 the school had an operating budget of slightly more than $250,000, by 1962 the overall budget of Little Rock University exceeded $6,000,000, and this increase in revenue allowed the institution to make the transition to a senior college with ease. As a reflection of increased funding, as early as 1957, the median salary for LRU faculty members for nine months rose to $5,127 from $4,470. The administration replaced the old system of paying summer session instructors on an enrollment basis with a more professional method of a set salary of 85 percent of the amount received by the instructor for nine weeks' employment during the fall or spring semester.[22]

The larger budget also resulted in campus improvements and new construction. For example, for over a decade since moving to the Hayes Street location, the college had operated without a permanent student union building. In November 1949, while the campus remained in an embryonic stage, John Larson had unsuccessfully urged the board of trustees to build a student center, and five years later the report of the

*Little Rock University's student union building. (1964 **Trojan**, 191)*

Ottenheimer Committee also called for the construction of a student union building with "student lounges, conference rooms, offices for the deans, yearbook office, cafeteria, [and a] dining room that might double as a ballroom."[23] Soon after the release of the committee's recommendations, Dean Brothers and business manager C.B. Pyles inspected student union buildings on campuses throughout Arkansas, observing features they hoped to incorporate into the new structure at Little Rock. In June 1956, school officials applied to the Federal Housing and Home Finance Agency for a $300,000 loan to build a student union facility. The administration anticipated repaying the loan from student fees and profits from the cafeteria, bookstore, and snack bar. Under President Stabler's direction, the college secured interim financing from several local banks in order to begin construction, and in March 1959 the Little Rock University student union building officially opened.

The structure bisected the old 33rd Street that once ran through the center of the campus. Its roof, designed by Robert H. Millett and Dietrick Neyland of the architectural firm of Ginocchio-Cromwell and Associates, was unusual — appearing to float over the building, and attacked by some critics as looking like a plowed field. The architects defended their creation by arguing that the roof made water drainage easier and improved the sound-reflecting properties of the rooms below.[24] The new building also included sunscreens on the east and west ends to reduce heat and glare; lattice work trimmed in chrome and blue; a general color scheme of coral, gray, and aqua; and adequate space for a bookstore, cafeteria and snack bar,

lounge, faculty dining room, and an open area that could be converted into a ballroom.

Before the building was finished, the administration hired Maybeth Deese Johnston as the new student union director and assistant to the dean of students. An alumna of LRJC and a recent graduate of the University of Arkansas, Mrs. Johnston assumed her duties in the summer of 1958 and served in various capacities connected with the student union for several years. Under her direction the LRU student union gave students a sense of school spirit that had been missing in the mid-1950s. Only a few months after the facility opened, the dean of students commented on how effective the union had been in aiding student morale and added that "this is a place where membership in a club or organization is not required — where students can gather with a minimum of supervision."[25]

Along with the student union, a split-level science building provided a major addition to the campus in 1959. Using money raised in the capital funds drive, school officials built the structure to house the biology, chemistry, botany, zoology, and physics departments on the north end of the college grounds. Constructed of brick with native stone retaining walls, the science building featured faculty offices and modern laboratories that included compressed air bottles, exhaust hoods, and lockers.[26]

On March 24, 1959, the administration hosted dedication ceremonies for the science facility and the student union building. Dr. W.E. Hanford, corporate vice-president for research for the Olin Mathieson Chemical Corporation of New York, delivered the dedicatory address

*James H. Penick (right), president of the Little Rock University Foundation, and Dr. William G. Cooper, Jr., president of the school's board of trustees, at the groundbreaking ceremony for LRU's new science building in 1958. (1958 **Trojan)***

The science building at LRU. (UALR Archives, Photo Collection 2, #98)

*Coleman Creek, longtime nemesis of LRJC and LRU students. (1965 **Trojan,** 72)*

to a crowd of over 500 guests. The addition of the new structures a decade after the construction of the basic campus in 1949 gave friends of LRU a sense their university had again become an institution "on the move" — a school destined to develop and expand far beyond the dreams of early supporters like John Larson and George Donaghey.

That optimism proved to be well-founded. Throughout the 1960s new construction projects became the hallmark of the Little Rock University campus. In March 1962 school officials completed a new home for the president of LRU at 5801 West 28th Street on the northern edge of the campus. The architects designed the red-brick, ranch-style home to accommodate various college functions as well as serving as a home for the future presidents of the institution.[27]

Carey Stabler, the first resident of the president's home, supervised the landscaping around the new house, just as he had tried to improve the overall appearance of the campus grounds. During the first semester of Stabler's presidency, school groundskeepers planted shrubbery and flowers throughout the main campus area, replaced broken window panes, and filled uneven places on the grounds with topsoil.[28]

In October 1960, the LRU board of trustees corrected one of the school's long-standing difficulties in this area by authorizing the appointment of Robert M. Staples as the institution's first full-time buildings and grounds superintendent.[29] The following spring Neil Park, a local landscape architect, submitted a long-range plan for the development of the campus, and school officials launched a comprehensive beau-

tification program that included paving roads and parking areas, creating a new entrance from University Avenue (the renamed Hayes Street), planting lawns and shrubs, and installing new tennis courts. The project cost almost $150,000 and generated an enthusiastic response from the student body, who, being commuters, expressed special gratitude for the resurfaced parking lots. The next step in the campus improvement campaign took place in the spring of 1964, when the administration, with federal financial assistance, constructed a long-needed bridge over Coleman Creek.[30]

Along with bridges, parking lots, and other areas of the physical plant, the college library also needed improvement. In the initial accreditation investigation by authorities from the North Central Association, the library received severe criticism, primarily because the facility's 30,000 volumes placed the school near the bottom of libraries with comparable student populations. For instance, Reed College of Portland, Oregon, with approximately 800 students, had over 107,000 books; Kenyon College in Ohio, with only 700 undergraduates, had a library with over 137,000 volumes. In 1958 the LRU board of trustees retained the services of Dr. Arthur McAnally, director of libraries at the University of Oklahoma, as a consultant to improve the overall quality of the Larson Memorial Library. McAnally reported that not only did the library have insufficient holdings, but also it needed additional staff, water fountains, restrooms, and more accessible book stacks.[31] Students, too, voiced dissatisfaction with the LRU library. In a post-graduation letter to President Stabler, one former student wrote, "I have truly enjoyed my two and a half years at Little Rock University. The only thing I have found inadequate is the library."[32]

In 1958 the librarian reported that the use of the library by students and faculty had risen by almost 60 percent from the previous year, mandating improved facilities. Soon after that, the administration and other supporters of the university began to work to improve the quality of the library. Following the construction of the new student union, the undergraduates ceased to regard the library as a social center, and according to one investigator from the North Central Association the "academic tone of the library substantially improved."[33] The general library budget rose from $10,300 in 1958-59 to $12,500 for 1959-60, and the following year J.D. Caskey assumed the position of head librarian, a post he held until resigning in 1963, when Hilda A. Elkins received an interim appointment to replace him.

In the meantime, the LRU library struggled to increase its total number of volumes. During the fall of 1959, the Little Rock chapter of the American Association of University Women conducted a book drive to aid the college's Larson Library. The members of the AAUW donated over 500 books from their own shelves and added an additional 2000 volumes and $850 in cash by soliciting donations from the community.[34] At about the same time Charles L. Thompson, an emeritus trustee of the Donaghey Foundation, died after willing his substantial personal library to the university. A year later, G.W. Blankenship contributed the major portion of his valuable Abraham Lincoln collection to LRU. Despite these gifts and the efforts

of the AAUW, however, the LRU library continued to lag behind other areas of the college as the institution developed into a respected small university.

Unlike the library, residence halls never became a reality at LRU, though the issue sparked later controversy. When Stabler assumed the presidency in 1956, he concurred with the board of trustees that LRU should avoid both football and dormitories. The LRU president later recalled that at that time he believed that "opposing dorms and football was promoting academics."[35] Less than two years later, though, Stabler modified his stand on residence halls. In January 1959 he informed the members of the college board that most urban colleges and universities had dormitories and "in order to develop to a full university and to reach our full capacity, residence halls appear to be advisable."[36] The college board sanctioned a series of studies on the issue in the early 1960s, but never reached complete agreement on the question. Ascertaining the demand for dormitories in Little Rock was difficult, since the majority of LRU students resided at home, and board members concluded they lacked a systematic method of measuring how many students from outside the capital city would seek admission if the school provided on-campus residence facilities. Throughout the institution's existence as Little Rock University the board of trustees and the administration discussed and debated the question, but failed to build any dormitories.

The creation of a board of trustees separate from the Little Rock School Board gave LRU a newfound sense of independence. At a meeting held on the LRU campus on July 29, 1959, the entire

Little Rock School Board voted to withdraw as the governing body of the university. The board had been under tremendous pressure since September 1957, when Arkansas Governor Orval E. Faubus precipitated a crisis over the racial integration of Little Rock Central High School. Since that time, the members of the school board had been consumed with court cases, dissatisfied parents, strife within the board, and the usual administrative duties of the group, along with the responsibilty for overseeing the development of the recently created senior college. Consequently the board cited "the heavy demands on our time made by the problems of school management for the Little Rock School District" as the official reason for withdrawing from the affairs of the college. To continue their work, the board appointed a new nine-person board of trustees to serve as the policy-making body of Little Rock University.

Although President Stabler and other supporters of the college had long advocated a separate board for LRU, the resignation of the school board generated a serious legal question as to whether or not the Donaghey Foundation, under the terms of the original trust, could continue to transfer funds to an institution not governed by the Little Rock School Board. To settle the issue university officials filed a lawsuit that reached the Supreme Court of Arkansas in 1960. In testimony before the court, school board member Russell H. Matson, Jr., indicated that when he ran for a position on the board he had no idea of the time or duties required of board members in governing the affairs of Little Rock University. Matson and Ted Lamb, another board member, each tes-

tified that their original intention had been to run for public school director, not university director, and that because of the pressing workload generated by the public schools, the board had inadequate time to deal with the problems of an expanding senior college.[37] Former school board chairman Foster Vineyard further stated that for several years "it was the unanimous feeling of the Directors ... that if there was a way for them to get rid of the responsibility [of making policy for LRU] they would be doing a service to the college."[38]

The overwhelming sentiment expressed by present and former school board members showed that the responsibility of governing the college had grown beyond the scope of the public school directors, and a separate board of trustees had become necessary to guarantee proper supervision and direction for LRU. On February 29, 1960, the state supreme court ruled by unanimous opinion that LRU could be operated by a private group of trustees without losing income from the Donaghey Foundation. In rendering the decision, Chief Justice Carlton Harris wrote that "it is apparent that Governor Donaghey could not, in 1929, have foreseen the conditions that made it almost impossible for the Little Rock School Board to operate the college. It is likewise apparent from his writings that the growth of LRU would have filled his heart and mind with pride and happiness."[39]

President Stabler regarded the acquisition of an independent board of trustees as a watershed in the school's history. On numerous occasions he pointed out that as long as the university's governing body remained the Little Rock School Board, the affairs of the institu-

*Richard C. Butler, the first chairman
of Little Rock University's independent
Board of Trustees in 1959. (1961 **Trojan)***

tion would always be of secondary importance, but with a separate board the membership could devote their full energies to the development of Little Rock University. While Stabler's assessment proved correct, the structure of the new board changed almost immediately. At the conclusion of the academic year in 1960, the trustees replaced the nine-person board with a fifteen-member board of trustees serving staggered six-year terms. Nominations for new trustees came from members of the Donaghey Foundation board, the school's alumni association, the Little Rock University Foundation, and the trustees themselves, with final selections being made by the full board. By 1962, the LRU board of trustees included five LRJC alumni — Richard C. Butler, Robert D. Lowry, E. Grainger Williams, Harold J. Engstrom, and Paul B. Jones — and represented the city's white, male ruling elite drawn almost exclusively from the business sector of the community. With the creation of a separate board, LRU gave up its unique status as a private institution under public control for the more traditional governing structure of most small, private colleges.

The reorganization of the board of trustees played a significant role in LRU's receiving full accreditation from the North Central Association in a remarkably brief period of time. In March 1958, even before the lines of authority for the college had been clarified, Stabler called a meeting of the faculty and instructed his teachers to begin collecting material for the self-study that would be a necessary part of the accreditation process. A few months later an outside consultant found that the thinking, activities, and general orientation of the

LRU teaching staff continued on a junior college level. In terms of budget, salaries, and facilities, the school's president felt that Little Rock University's case for quick accreditation might be inadequate. The North Central investigating team, however, admired the university's potential, acknowledged the importance of the independent trustees, and liked the spirit of cooperation between the faculty and the administration.[40] As a result, on April 6, 1960, representatives of the North Central Association of Colleges and Secondary Schools officially informed President Stabler that the association had voted to accredit Little Rock University as a full senior institution.[41] Upon receiving the decision, Stabler commented that "we consider full accreditation a commencement of all the ambitious programs that we have planned for the University," and the school's president immediately called a special assembly to announce the accreditation to the LRU student body. At that meeting Donaghey Foundation president John Rule, cognizant of the recent years of turmoil in the capital city, told the audience that "my first thought after hearing this news was 'Thank God, something good has finally happened to Little Rock.'"[42] In a congratulatory letter, Dr. Irwin J. Lubbers, the president of Hope College in Michigan and a member of the North Central group, echoed the newfound optimism: "I trust that this recognition will be a further impetus to great achievement on one of the most exciting campuses in the country."[43]

In less than five years the declining morale that marked the junior college in the mid-1950s had disappeared and had been replaced by a spirit of exhilaration

Harold Engstrom, longtime member of
the institution's board of trustees (1956
Trojan)

that carried into the 1960s. A large part of this change resulted from the efforts of President Stabler. One faculty member, recalling these years of transition, said, "Stabler was a great man. He was just the man we needed."[44] Stabler built strong ties with the local community and developed an attitude among Little Rock business leaders that they should regard LRU as their school — an institution contributing to the growth of their city. The same instructor who spoke of Stabler as a great man also told one interviewer that the school's president "knew how to get along with the businessmen downtown. He spoke their language. He played tennis and he liked to do social things that would be good for the school. Without Stabler we would never be where we are today."[45] Several individuals connected with the institution helped Stabler bridge the gap between the college and the community. Richard Butler donated his membership in the Riverdale Country Club for the use of the school's president and his family,[46] while other supporters of the school helped elect Stabler to the presidency of the downtown Rotary Club in 1965.

Business manager Francis L. Robinson said that Stabler "had a very steady, modest approach, and that was what was needed when he came here."[47] Between 1957 and 1963 that modest approach helped transform the college in Little Rock from a demoralized, factionalized, and floundering institution into an accredited and expanding senior college destined to become an important factor in the history of education in Arkansas. Aided by a group of dedicated students and faculty members, the LRU community therefore entered the 1960s

with high hopes of making what President Stabler called "our own peculiar contribution to the general idea of higher education in the nation."[48]

CHAPTER TEN

"A Song That's Ever New," 1957-1963

*A*fter 30 years as a junior college, the institution John Larson founded in the north wing of the local high school began operations as Little Rock University in September 1957. Between then and 1963, the school experienced a dynamic period of change highlighted by the addition of new faculty members, expanded student life, increased enrollment, the return of varsity athletics, and an effort by the entire academic community to redefine the mission of the institution as LRU emerged in a new role as a modern urban college.

The faculty assumed a position of leadership in the new senior institution. The initial investigating team from the North Central Association reported that "one of the greatest strengths of Little Rock University is the alertness, vigor, and enthusiasm of the faculty and staff. The faculty is youthful, but seems to sense a burgeoning future for the university, to which they are quite dedicated."[1] The North Central representatives did recognize some weaknesses in the new school's teaching staff. Their official report said that only 11 of 45 full-time faculty members held a doctorate and commented that "by some usual standards the faculty would rank low."[2] Dr. C.W. Kreger, an outside consultant,

echoed the findings of the North Central Committee. While admiring the dedication of the LRU teachers, Kreger also told President Stabler that "it will not be easy to change the thinking of your present staff with respect to academic standards ... from the junior college level to the senior college level."[3] Kreger further recommended that the administration immediately hire as many new faculty members as possible who held a doctorate and had experience teaching at a four-year school.

Although Stabler agreed with Kreger that LRU needed to expand the school's instructional staff, he wanted to maintain an emphasis on teaching rather than on faculty research — a choice far too often avoided by college administrators. Stabler told the board of trustees that "faculty promotions too often are based on how much people publish and not much credit is given for great teaching. I think you must have some people on a college staff who are teachers and not researchers."[4] Stabler devoted considerable time to assembling the new faculty for the college, although the task often proved difficult. By 1960 the school's chief executive reported that after corresponding with 20 professional placement bureaus, 30 graduate placement offices, and numerous deans and

*Dean Harold I. Woolard. (1958 **Trojan**)*

division chairmen throughout the country, he found that the number of college instructors available had decreased appreciably in the last two years.[5] To complicate the recruiting process even more, Stabler recalled later, "I could have filled every position two or three times with local people ... so the problem was not filling every position with a University of Arkansas graduate. Actually," he added, "we yielded a good bit on this."[6]

In LRU's early years as a four-year institution, part of the difficulty in finding qualified instructors resulted from the school's inability to pay adequate salaries to attract scholars from outside Arkansas. By 1961, however, Stabler reported that the median salary at Little Rock University for nine months had risen to $6,097 from only $4,470 in 1957 and told one member of the board of trustees that LRU paid "as good salaries as the average private institution of the United States."[7] With the improving pay scale and the addition of new faculty members, the administration assigned academic rank to the instructional staff for the first time in the school's history. Starting in the fall of 1959, all full-time teachers received a rank of either professor, associate professor, assistant professor, or instructor based on their degrees, years of teaching experience, and effectiveness in instruction and research. According to the dean of the university, the LRU faculty accepted this change in good spirit as a necessary part of a four-year program.[8] The administration wanted the ranking system primarily because of the rapid expansion of the LRU teaching staff. In 1957 the school had only 26 full-time instructors, only two of whom held the Ph.D. degree. By

1963 LRU had 50 full-time teachers with 25 percent holding the doctorate and another 25 percent in the process of attaining it.

This new faculty included some excellent teachers, some good scholars, and a few individuals who combined both qualities and remained a part of the institution for over a quarter of a century. With the retirement of Dean Brothers in 1957, Dr. Nicholas W. Quick, a former assistant to the president at Texas A&M, became dean of the faculty and director of the evening division. Quick also administered a graduate placement service to help students find careers with local companies. In the fall of 1957 Dr. Harold I. Woolard, a former dean at Upper Iowa University, became the registrar and dean of students, and in January 1958 the administration appointed him chairman of the Division of Humanities. When Quick left LRU in 1960, Woolard became dean of the university and played a major role in directing the school's academic program throughout the remainder of the decade.

During the institution's first year as a senior college other instructors joined the LRU teaching staff, several of whom remained at the school into the 1980s. In the chemistry department, Billie G. Broach and Dr. Wilson J. Broach began their long and distinguished careers at the institution in 1957, as did Donald L. Warmack, a former student at the Juilliard School of Music, who later became the head of LRU's fine arts department. They joined Richard Dixon, a historian and LRJC graduate, who had become a member of the staff a few years earlier, in smoothing the transition to senior level status. In 1958 Dr. Dudley S. Beard joined the LRU community as

History instructor Richard Dixon.
*(1956 **Trojan**)*

registrar and assistant director of the evening division. Over the next 30 years Beard also taught sociology, coached the LRU golf team, and earned considerable recognition as an excellent amateur golfer. Also in 1958 Dr. Everett L. Edmondson, a former head of educational research at Arizona State College, became the director of LRU's education program; a year later Barbara B. Taegel became LRU's first dean of women.

In 1960 Dr. Calvin R. Ledbetter, Jr., joined the faculty and soon became one of the college's most recognizable figures. Over the next three decades Ledbetter won a seat in the state legislature, published numerous scholarly works, and served in several top administrative positions as the university expanded and later became part of the University of Arkansas system. In the early 1960s several other distinguished scholars and teachers became a part of LRU's academic staff, including Rose Berry in elementary education; Richard Frothingham in philosophy and religion; Gene G. McCoy, Robert Culpepper, and Lloyd Bowie in the business school; Bedford Hadley in history; James F. Butler in economics; and Roslyn Donald in English.

Meeting regularly on the first Wednesday of each month, these and other faculty members began the process of establishing Little Rock University as a respected senior college. Although often concerned with issues relating to faculty welfare like group hospitalization and life insurance plans, the instructors' main focus in LRU's early years remained improving educational opportunities for the students of central Arkansas.

To achieve that goal, the faculty, in co-operation with the administration, made several changes in the operations of the institution. In 1957, the school abandoned the three-point grading system for a method that gave four points for an A, three for a B, two for a C, and one for a D. In 1959 school officials shifted the department of economics to the business school, dropped the vocational aviation program, and inaugurated a bachelor's degree in medical technology in cooperation with the University of Arkansas Medical Center and a similar program with St. Vincent's Infirmary. The next year LRU's leadership established a program under which a student who completed a three-year pre-law curriculum could receive a bachelor's degree from Little Rock University upon the subsequent completion of the first year of law school. Although the institution maintained two-year certificate programs in drafting, engineering technician, laboratory technician, and secretarial training, by 1960 the major emphasis of the school had clearly shifted to a four-year bachelor's program.

Consequently, 1960 became a pivotal year in the early development of LRU, when the faculty and the administration completely reorganized the academic program, enabling LRU to offer bachelor of arts or science degrees in eight areas of study rather than five under the previous structure. School officials created two new divisions — the Division of Fine Arts and the Division of Applied Arts and Continuing Education — and subdivided the former Division of Natural Sciences into the Division of Biological Sciences and the Division of Physical Science and Mathematics.[9] These divisions joined the Divisions of Business Administration and Economics, Hu-

Dr. Calvin R. Ledbetter, Jr., professor of political science, chairman of the political science department, and later dean of the College of Liberal Arts. (UALR News Bureau Photos, Nov./Dec. '65, Roll O)

manities, Teacher Education, and Social Science to give the students of Little Rock University a well-organized curriculum and provide the teaching staff with well-defined lines of authority. Although the system underwent minor modifications in 1963, the realignment made in 1960 remained the basic academic organization until the merger with the University of Arkansas in 1969.

Despite the divisional reorganization in 1960, the general objectives of LRU were essentially the same as those of Little Rock Junior College — to provide a chance for young people to develop culturally and intellectually in an academic environment. The LRU *Bulletin* of 1962-63 defined the school's aims as offering the students the opportunity for self-development "not only in preparation for chosen professions and vocations but also for general education, by which is meant an understanding of the various fields of knowledge and the discipline of learning."[10] The last point proved to be especially important as LRU expanded in the 1960s. With the democratization of higher education, "people's colleges" like Little Rock University experienced increasing pressure to provide vocational education. As a result, in the years after 1960 programs in business administration, engineering, and teacher education increased, often at the expense of traditional liberal arts studies. To preserve the ideals of general education, several members of the LRU faculty fought to maintain the liberal arts as the foundation of the college's curriculum. They recognized that a program strong in literature, languages, mathematics, history, art, religion, philosophy, psychology, sociology, and the natural sciences prepared students to live and

not just to earn a living. As the university expanded, however, the efforts of those instructors often met with resistance from colleagues who, unfortunately, could not tell the difference between education and training.

Both advocates and opponents of the liberal arts recognized that older and narrower concepts of the functions of a college had become inadequate, and most of the LRU faculty proved willing to experiment with innovative programs designed to expand the horizons of the student body. Drawing on the resources of the Little Rock community, the college began offering a unique series of courses. In 1962, for example, Dr. Stuart Eurman, the director of the Metropolitan Area Planning Commission (Metroplan) taught a course in "Urban Problems and Planning," while Elton Donaubauer, a former director of the Pulaski County United Fund, taught a course entitled "Community Agencies and Services."[11]

LRU personnel also became involved in several pioneering efforts to use television for instructional purposes in Arkansas. When educational television made its debut in the state in 1957 with a series of programs on station KTHV dealing with the Dead Sea Scrolls, Harold Woolard of the college served as the discussion leader.[12] LRU faculty members became further involved in educational television in the fall of 1958 when executives from KTHV gave the school 30 minutes of free air time each Sunday afternoon to produce a program for the cultural enrichment of the community. Following a spirited debate among the instructors regarding the wisdom of the new senior college's assuming such a responsibility,[13] "Little Rock University Speaks" became the first con-

*Inside the Larson Memorial Library in 1959. (1959 **Trojan**, 45)*

tinuous local educational television program in Arkansas.[14] Hosted by Bob Fuller of the KTHV staff, the program featured panels of students asking questions of experts in several fields of interest to the citizens of the state. Although the show proved relatively popular with the viewing public, the college discontinued "Little Rock University Speaks" in April 1959 because of a conflict with the host station over schedules.[15]

The following spring the college faculty resumed an active involvement in educational television by participating in the "Continental Classroom," a series of programs on "Physics in the Atomic Age" presented on the National Broadcasting Company network under a grant by the Ford Foundation. Aired for 30 minutes, five days a week, the Continental Classroom included seminars on Saturdays led by an LRU instructor and gave students the opportunity to earn four semester-hours of college credit.[16]

Unfortunately, not all of the university's innovative efforts proved as successful as the experiments in educational television. After several years of study, evaluation, and cooperative effort, LRU officials' plan to offer a joint bachelor of fine arts degree with the Arkansas Arts Center failed to materialize because of a negative reaction by representatives of the North Central Association.[17] An attempt to establish a reserve officers training program on campus met with a similar fate. Soon after the college received full accreditation, President Stabler made overtures to the Department of the Navy in hopes of securing a unit of the Naval Reserve Officers Training Corps for LRU. A spokesman for the Navy informed Stabler that, although the original Naval ROTC had been es-

tablished in 1925 to supplement the U.S. Naval Academy as a source of career officers, since 1946 only one new NROTC group had been added to a total of 52 and the need for officers did not justify establishing any new units.[18] Undaunted, Stabler tried to interest the Army and the Air Force in locating officer's training centers at LRU, but discovered that both branches of the armed forces operated these programs under nonexpansion policies in the early 1960s. The inability of LRU to offer a cooperative degree with the Arts Center and to acquire an ROTC unit illustrated the difficulty encountered by newer institutions of higher education in establishing their viability and competing with older colleges and universities, where such programs were well-established traditions.

To offset these problems and to build credibility, recently founded schools like Little Rock University concentrated on areas in which the college could excel. Since one of LRU's most important functions was educating older students, immediately after securing senior college status the administration expanded the coursework offered by the college's evening division. As early as September 1957, the *Arkansas Democrat* reported that at LRU "there is an ever widening group of students going into night classes on the junior level — men and women who have full time jobs, have had two years of college and want to get their degrees."[19]

Aware of accusations that evening classes often produced substandard education, Dean Quick made a concerted effort to assure prospective students that, at LRU, night school classes maintained the same quality as those that met during regular school hours. "We interview and counsel with each new evening faculty member," Quick told a newspaper reporter in 1957. "We want to dispel any 'watered-down' concept of evening education."[20] During the 1957-58 school year the evening division faculty included only seven full-time university instructors and 27 part-time teachers, but over the next several years the administration steadily increased the number of regular professors in the night school. Under Dean Quick's direction, the school began using division chairmen to counsel undergraduates at night school registration to prevent students from taking random, unrelated courses that would not fulfill desired degree requirements. These older students who returned to school, often while working at full-time jobs, tended to be mature and conscientious about their studies. Furnishing these individuals with the opportunity to earn a college degree became one of LRU's most important contributions as Arkansas's "people's college."

The expansion of the night school program fit into a general pattern of community service provided by Little Rock University as a continuation of a tradition begun during the school's junior college years. One of LRU's public relation's slogans of the early 1960s declared that "a great city requires a great university." From the beginning of the school, the citizens of Little Rock supported the institution, and after the change to a senior college that support became even stronger. Following his retirement as president of the university, Carey Stabler recalled that "every year I was greatly pleased at the public support. I greeted my faculty each September

with the same old phrase — I think the honeymoon is still on. That's the way the city treated you."[21]

While the Little Rock community aided the college by contributing to fund-raising campaigns and book drives, hiring students, and enrolling in classes, LRU offered the city an increasing number of special educational programs and cultural activities. In 1957 the college sponsored a workshop for business education teachers that was the first of its kind in the South to teach a new method of note-taking called "Briefhand."[22] Five years later, LRU initiated an annual series of small business management development seminars designed to help owners and managers of businesses solve administrative problems.[23] Also in the early 1960s, the university sponsored district science fairs for local junior and senior high school students; co-sponsored the "Great Decisions" programs along with organizations like the League of Women Voters; and offered numerous courses designed to meet the needs of local industries.[24]

LRU also contributed to a cultural reawakening in Little Rock in the 1960s. Divided by racial strife for several years, the citizens of the city welcomed expanding opportunities to enjoy art, drama, and music provided by both LRU and the Arkansas Arts Center. As early as 1957 a critic for the *Arkansas Gazette*, in praising a recital by violinist Donald Warmack and pianist Margaret Warmack of the college faculty, wrote that "the Little Rock University Department of Music gives promise of filling an active and important role in the cultural life of the city."[25] The college built on that beginning by sponsoring other recitals, dramatic productions, art exhibits, and the Junior League Art Center, an on-campus project that received financial support from the Little Rock chapter of the Junior League.[26]

To further LRU's community service function, President Stabler, in his first report to the board of trustees, suggested that a program of concerts or lectures would enhance the college's reputation as a center of culture in central Arkansas.[27] In 1962 the school acted on the president's idea and instituted a series of lectures entitled "Evenings at Eight." For several years, under the direction of a steering committee headed by Mrs. Merlin Moore, Little Rock University presented a series of addresses by nationally noted authors and used the proceeds from the programs to benefit the Larson Memorial Library. Arkansas Senator John McClellan discussed his book *Crime Without Punishment* for the inaugural lecture, and other speakers during the 1962-63 school year included publisher Bennett Cerf, White House correspondent Merrian Smith, author Bergen Evans, and actor Vincent Price.

The citizens of Little Rock supported "Evenings at Eight" with enthusiasm. At the conclusion of the first year's program the editor of the campus newspaper wrote that the series had "distinguished our school immensely. Probably no college our size in the South can boast a more erudite roster of speakers during the last year."[28] Over the ensuing years, LRU's "Evenings at Eight" brought quality speakers like journalist Cleveland Amory, architect Albert Mayer, linguist S.I. Hayakawa, and novelists Jesse Hill Ford and Gore Vidal to Little Rock. Unfortunately, the high fees charged by prominent writers prevented the program from generating

the needed funds for the library, and poor attendance at the lectures by LRU students forced school officials to cancel "Evenings at Eight" during the latter part of the decade.

Not all of LRU's community service efforts involved bringing culture to the capital city. In 1959, officials at the college quietly aided dozens of local high school students who had been displaced as a result of the Little Rock integration crisis. On September 2, 1957, Governor Faubus had ordered the Arkansas National Guard to surround the campus of Central High School, and two days later the guardsmen had refused to allow nine black students to enter the school. Only under the supervision of the 101st Airborne Infantry Division of the United States Army did desegregation come to the city's high schools in 1957-58. The following year, fear and hysteria led citizens of the community to vote to close all of the city's high schools, denying several hundred students the chance to complete their secondary education.

To accommodate some of those individuals, LRU officials initiated a program to admit certain candidates to the college even though they had not graduated from high school. Applicants had to have fifteen academic units from an accredited high school or a combination of school and correspondence work and a passing grade on a college entrance examination. Under these provisions more than 90 students gained admission to Little Rock University for the spring semester in January 1959, thereby gaining the chance to continue their education despite the controversy that plagued the city's public school system.[29]

The events of the late 1950s and the growing civil rights movement in the

The Fine Arts classroom building, later known as Stabler Hall. (1967 **Trojan,** *97)*

early 1960s also forced Little Rock University officials to examine the racial policies of their own institution. However, the leadership of LRU, like other segments of the Little Rock community, refused to make rapid changes. Article II of the school's constitution provided that the purpose of Little Rock University was to "promote generally the higher education of white persons," and the LRU board of trustees refused to alter that policy for seven years following the 1957 crisis at Central High School. Finally, in the spring of 1964, President Stabler presented the question of allowing black students to attend LRU at a faculty meeting. Although the idea met some opposition, the final consensus of the instructional staff, according to one teacher, "was that this was a thing that was going to come ... and we owed it to the blacks to have an opportunity."[30] The following August, the school's board of trustees, fearful that the government would not allow LRU to continue participating in federal financial aid programs, followed the lead of the faculty and removed the segregation clause from the school's constitution.[31]

By the opening of classes in September 1964, the administration had adopted an official policy that prohibited "discrimination based on race or color in eligibility for courses, lectures, in classroom seating, or access to dining halls."[32] Ten black students chose to register for the fall semester.[33] That number increased steadily over the next few years and by 1967, almost 200 blacks attended LRU, justly fulfilling the institution's role as a "people's college." The inclusion of black undergraduates in the mid-1960s changed the character of what had remained an essentially homo-

geneous student body for over 30 years.

Since the transition from Little Rock Junior College to LRU the student body had been increasing. In the fall of 1958, 1,364 students (89 seniors, 204 juniors, 323 sophomores, and 654 freshmen) enrolled at LRU, and by 1962 the total enrollment reached 1,780. During that period male students outnumbered females (1,133 males and 647 coeds registered in 1958), and approximately 95 percent of the student body came from central Arkansas. In 1960, for example, 382 LRU students had attended Central High in Little Rock; 160 came from North Little Rock; 89 attended Hall High in Little Rock; and less than 200 undergraduates came from outside Arkansas.[34]

Recognizing that most LRU students came from similar backgrounds, the administration attempted to make the student body more cosmopolitan. In 1962 President Stabler told one member of the board of trustees, "LRU urgently needs some foreign students for they are usually superior, brilliant students .... They should contribute greatly to the academic and social life of LRU."[35] The members of the board agreed and in September 1962 provided full scholarships for two Latin Americans, who traveled to Little Rock under the sponsorship of the local Rotary Club.

LRU students, like their junior college forerunners, were still working their way through school. One survey conducted by the registrar's office after the creation of LRU revealed that 84 percent of the male students and 20 percent of the females worked at least part-time. Most students had to work in order to finance their education. By and large the students agreed with one LRU undergraduate who told a reporter that "when

*LRU intramurals, 1963. (1964 **Trojan)***

you work your way through college, you become aware of monetary values, and most important, the value of a college education."[36]

The LRU student body also tended to be Protestant. A comprehensive profile assembled in the late 1950s showed that 33 percent of LRU students were Baptist, 21.5 percent Methodist, and 7.2 percent Presbyterian. Less than 9 percent were Jewish or Catholic. Unlike students at more traditional residential colleges, LRU students tended to be married. Between 1958 and 1962 approximately 40 percent of the LRU student body had spouses, while 68 percent of the graduating classes of 1961 and 1962 were married.[37] The high percentage of married students resulted partly from the fact that LRU undergraduates also tended to be older than their counterparts who attended residential schools. In 1962 LRU students averaged 24 years of age (28.8 years at graduation), a fact that gave the college's student body one of its unique characteristics. Returning to school to prepare for a better job or to improve the quality of their lives, these students again and again dispelled the myth that older people cannot learn as well as younger ones. In the early 1960s the *Arkansas Gazette* highlighted a trio of female students, all well into their thirties, who laughingly regarded themselves as members of the "Old Timers Club" or the "Delayed Education Club." Despite pressures from family obligations and initial uncertainty about their abilities, each woman had become an honor student at the college and represented an important segment of the LRU student body.[38]

Partly because of the presence of so many older students, LRU undergrad-

uates tended to major in practical rather than theoretical courses of study. A survey of degrees conferred between 1959 and 1964 indicated that the majority of LRU students majored in business administration or teacher education. In 1961, for example, 41 students received degrees in business administration, while only 8 majored in social sciences. That same year 16 graduated in teacher education in comparison to 10 students in humanities and 2 in fine arts.

Although LRU students were slightly older than their counterparts at residential colleges, the undergraduates attending the Little Rock campus enjoyed a full range of student activities. Soon after the establishment of the senior college, the editor of the campus newspaper expressed a sense of excitement regarding the new school and its possibilities. "Being included in a pioneer venture," he wrote, "is like a sail around the world with Magellan .... The expanding of a college is something interesting and being a part of the expansion is like no other feeling."[39]

Campus life sustained that sense of excitement as former Little Rock Junior College institutions changed or disappeared and new traditions and activities began to replace them. In April 1961 the LRU students, in a special election, voted to change the name of the campus newspaper from the *Chatter* to the *Forum*, rejecting alternatives like the *Spectator* and the *Sentinel*.[40] A year earlier the college adopted a new alma mater featuring music by Margaret Warmack and Glenn Metcalf of the school's music department and lyrics by junior Rosemary Hester:

We lift our hearts and voices in a song

*The 1965 Miss LRU Contest. (1965 **Trojan**, 104)*

that's ever new—
With a love that never falters we will
serve thee, LRU—
Time will come when we must leave you,
part and go our separate ways,
But to thee we will be true, our Alma
Mater, L-R-U.

Little Rock University students initiated several other new activities during the institution's early years as a senior college. Before the return of varsity basketball, several campus organizations co-sponsored a homecoming carnival with booths, old-fashioned melodramas, and a dance, and for a few years the annual fraternity-faculty March of Dimes basketball game was one of the social highlights of the college year. More popular than the charity benefit game, the annual Trojan Beauty Contest sponsored by the Student Government Association evolved into the Miss LRU Contest, which allowed the winning coed to compete for the titles of Miss Arkansas and — it was hoped — Miss America. In the early 1960s, popular radio announcer Brother Hal emceed the LRU pageant, which, according to one critic who felt the contest demeaned women students, rewarded "boobs instead of brains."[41]

With the rise of new activities, several traditions from the institution's junior college days faded into the background of campus life. Although school leaders continued to hold Donaghey Day each spring, attendance dwindled, and in 1963 the chairman of the faculty social committee recommended that the administration retitle the event "Founder's Day."[42] That same year reference to Stunt Night, once the most successful LRJC social activity, disappeared from the college *Bulletin*, and efforts to continue the All-School Picnic failed to generate much enthusiasm by the mid-1960s.

On the other hand, Phi Theta Kappa, the Jaycee honor group for students in the upper ten percent of the freshmen and sophomore classes, continued as the most prestigious honor society for several years after the change to a four-year school, even though new groups founded at LRU in 1961 like Alpha Kappa Psi, the business honorary organization, and Sword and Shield, a senior college honor society, gradually replaced Phi Theta Kappa. With the increase in enrollment, other clubs and student organizations expanded to meet the varied needs of LRU undergraduates. In 1961 Circle K, a Kiwanis-sponsored service organization, became active on the campus, and in 1963 Quindecim, another men's service club, gained official recognition from the administration. Hood and Tassel and Sigma Tau Lambda provided similar activities for women students. By 1963 the university offered interested students a debate club, a chess club, an investment club, a choir, a theater group, political clubs, and academic-social clubs in virtually every discipline within the institution.[43] Occasionally involvement in student activities, however, presented difficulties to both the students and the faculty. In 1960, the dean of the university reported that requests for authorized student absences threatened to become a problem. "Class time lost to participate in field trips, contests, and meetings of student organizations," he wrote, "can easily be a threat to academic standards."[44]

Greek letter social fraternities and sororities, too, played an increasingly important role at LRU. At the beginning of the fall term in 1961, President Stabler

*Fraternity hijinks. (1959 **Trojan)***

wrote a member of the board of trustees that "the students and public are making constant inquiries as to the earliest date on which local fraternity and sorority groups may petition for affiliation with a national fraternity or sorority."[45] Stabler believed national social clubs would help student morale on the LRU campus, and his administration developed a reputation for being friendly to the Greek system. The faculty followed Stabler's lead in the matter and recommended "affiliation with national fraternities and sororities as an advisable and desirable thing for Little Rock University."[46] School officials communicated with the national headquarters of various Greek letter organizations to determine the policies of each group, and in 1963 five local clubs affiliated with national organizations: Beta Chi, which had originally been the Battlecriers, became a chapter of Phi Beta Phi; Tau Sigma, a local sorority founded in 1960, became Delta Delta Delta; Zeta Phi joined the Kappa Kappa Gamma organization; Delta Kappa switched to Sigma Nu; and Chi Sigma Epsilon, a men's group that grew out of an independent intramural team called the "Hot Dogs," joined Kappa Sigma. A few years earlier, Phi Alpha Beta, the oldest social club on the campus, had affiliated with Phi Lambda Chi to form the first national social fraternity at LRU, but administrative pressure in 1961 forced the local club to sever ties with the national fraternity[47] and a few years later the group became a colony of Sigma Alpha Epsilon. Most students recalled their relationships with their fraternity or sorority in terms of friendships, parties, or scenes like the one described in a 1967 issue of the *Forum*: "After the smokers and propa-

ganda sessions are over, the bids are given out through the Dean of Men. Pledges traditionally come charging out of the field house, running each other down, and join with the fraternity groups who have gathered outside to greet the new and welcomed pledges. Then all groups enter the Student Union and engage in a noise making contest of fraternity cheers."[48]

Occasionally the fraternities reflected more than the adolescent need for peer companionship and became an embarrassment to the university. In 1962 LRU's dean of men placed the Kappa Sigs on probation following a fraternity dance at the Marion Hotel during which members of the group became intoxicated, vandalized hotel property, and engaged in a fist fight resulting in several Kappa Sigs' requiring medical treatment.[49] The probation also resulted from the destruction of property in an LRU classroom where the organization conducted weekly meetings. Among other things, the fraternity men destroyed a collection of art projects made by primary schoolchildren and loaned to the college to be used for demonstration purposes in education classes. In an irate letter to the dean, Everett L. Edmondson of the education department demanded disciplinary action against the Kappa Sigs and asked if "you can imagine how the little children will feel when they see how LRU has 'cared' for their treasures."[50]

Not all fraternity activities required disciplinary measures. The annual Sigma Nu Relays featured slapstick competition among the school's sororities in events like egg tosses, the "Tubby Tube Race," and a tug-of-war over a mud pit. Some Greek groups sponsored dances,

*Racing for the honor of "Miss Tubby Tube" at the Sigma Nu relays during the 1968-69 school year. (1969 **Trojan)***

hayrides, and Christmas parties, and others engaged in humanitarian undertakings like an Easter egg hunt for the orphans of the nearby Methodist Children's Home, a clothing drive for prison inmates, and a Christmas party for patients at the Arkansas Children's Hospital. The national Greek letter societies provided a good deal of harmless collegiate fun for the commuter-oriented LRU students, but never dominated campus politics or social life as they did at schools like the University of Arkansas in the early 1960s.

The return of varsity basketball became another important element in the student life at LRU during its transition to a senior college, despite early opposition from President Stabler. Although Stabler had a strong background in sports, having attended the University of Alabama on a football-basketball scholarship, he had soured on the value of college athletics by the time he assumed the presidency of LRU. Between 1956 and 1960, the faculty and board of trustees believed, as he did, that a deemphasis of athletics promoted academics. In 1960, though, the school's president and some members of the board changed their minds on the issue after several editorials and petitions reflected strong student support for varsity athletics at LRU. That summer, the trustees voted to reestablish intercollegiate basketball with scholarship players at Little Rock University after five years of inactivity. The decision followed a positive vote by the students to assess an activity fee to help finance the new athletic program.[51]

Stabler and some board members wanted to hire Lawrence Mobley, a successful former coach at Little Rock Cen-

tral High School, to be the new Trojan mentor, but Mobley accepted a similar position at his alma mater, Hendrix College in Conway.[52] The LRU administration then hired Bill Ballard to fill a dual role as dean of men and head basketball coach. Because of his winning record and positive attitude, Ballard, a former athlete and coach at the College of the Ozarks in Clarksville, immediately raised the hopes of LRU supporters that the school could again field respectable athletic teams. On November 4, 1960, varsity basketball returned to the campus when a Ballard-coached team under the name of the LRU Independents defeated the Pottsville Independents 67-59 in double overtime behind Brooks Nash's sixteen points, and for the remainder of the season the team competed in the local Amateur Athletic Union league in preparation for intercollegiate play the following year. The 1961-62 Trojans, despite a lack of size, experience, and ability, played a full schedule of games against small college teams primarily from Arkansas and, although they won only six games, earned a reputation as a "scrappy, hustling bunch."[53] Led by players like Freddy Eastin, John Narkinsky, Larry Finley, David Cone, Billy Clark, and Naymon Mallett, the Trojans received strong support from the LRU students, causing President Stabler to comment that "apparently the student body has a keen interest in the renewal of intercollegiate athletics at the University."[54]

The LRU basketball teams of the early 1960s drew adequate crowds and helped student morale by providing a focus for Homecoming and other social activities. In 1963 the school's president proclaimed "Trojan Triumph Week," which

174

*A display of school spirit, revived by the reestablishment of Trojan basketball in the early 1960s. (1963 **Trojan,** 15)*

*Basketball coach Bill Ballard (left) discussing strategy with players Don Hurst (22), Freddie Eastin, and assistant coach Cleve Branscum during the 1964 season. (1964 **Trojan**)*

included a campus pep rally and a caravan through downtown Little Rock to promote interest in LRU athletics. Ballard also initiated a successful annual high school basketball tournament during the Christmas holidays to help scout propects for future teams, and the addition of players like Don Hurst, Roger Armburst, Bob Dobson, Alvin Corder, Tommy Louks, and Ronnie Hubbard enabled the Trojans to win the Dixie Tournament in Memphis three years in a row and to post several respectable seasons in the early and mid-1960s. The modest success of the basketball team capped an era of growth for Little Rock University. The remainder of the decade proved to be a time of both consolidation and even more expansion, leading to the eventual merger with the University of Arkansas in 1969. In the meantime, LRU officials built buildings, added faculty members, worked to earn an academic reputation, and weathered one of the most turbulent eras in the history of American higher education — the late 1960s.

C H A P T E R   E L E V E N

"Last Resort University"

*I*n February 1963 the editor of LRU's student newspaper, the *Forum*, voiced a difficulty that haunted the college for the remainder of the decade. "Like Sir Lancelot LRU needs a cause," he wrote. "The University of Arkansas looks for football players, Arkansas State seeks university status, Harding hopes to preserve the American Way of Life, Hendrix and Ouachita advocate the Christian Way of Life. But LRU, beloved LRU, doesn't have a single banner to wave."[1] The writer was right: Little Rock University lacked a positive identity within the hierarchy of higher education in the state. Between 1963 and 1969 the search for that individuality provided one of the major themes in the institution's development. Following the opening of Little Rock University, the students, faculty, and administration struggled to win respectability for the new senior college — a task that sometimes proved difficult. As late as 1963, five years after the founding of LRU, for instance, a group of horrified Little Rock University students discovered that the school's pennant that flew alongside the flags of other colleges in the city's War Memorial Stadium still read "LRJC."

To build a positive image, LRU supporters attempted to portray their institution as the state's only urban university. At a meeting of the national Association of Urban Universities in 1968, however, the delegates defined a true urban institution, as opposed to simply a college located in a city, as one dedicated to solving the social, economic, and other problems that plagued America's cities. President Stabler of LRU, who attended the meeting, quickly pointed out that neither LRU's budget nor its institutional aims permitted a commitment of time, staff, physical facilities, and money to a direct attack on economic and other urban problems.[2] Rejecting the idea of becoming an urban university defined in that way, Little Rock University officials then concentrated on doing the same thing the college had always done — providing basic educational opportunities for citizens of the greater Little Rock area — and hoped that from that commitment a positive identity could be forged.

An important element in that new identity centered on LRU as the fastest-growing institution of higher education in the state. Throughout the 1960s, as the baby boomer generation reached college age, the school's enrollment increased again and again, generating an almost desperate need for new facilities. In the fall of 1963, over 2100 undergraduates registered for classes, representing a 20-percent increase in enrollment over the previous fall. Since school officials had anticipated only a 15-percent rise, overcrowding became a way of life at the college. "Enrollment at LRU has outgrown facilities," the *Arkansas Democrat* reported. "Classrooms are packed, laboratories are overtaxed, and the library is cramped."[3] Students and teachers complained of traffic jams and inadequate parking areas and the registrar's office cited the loss of a number of qualified students, who, despite the administration's efforts to add classes and move extra chairs into some classrooms, could not make a satisfactory schedule. The spring semester of 1964 offered no relief, as enrollment increased 20 percent over the previous spring and overcrowded conditions continued. By that time the growth rate for the college reached twice the national average rate for similar institutions; while Little Rock University was one of 20 colleges in Arkansas, 20 percent of the entire state's increase in college enrollment took place at LRU.[4] The 1964 fall enrollment reached 2,489 students and only the addition of fifteen new faculty members and a schedule that included noon and midday classes enabled the administration to accommodate the record number of students.

In response to the rapid increase in the student body, school authorities inaugurated a $1.5 million fund-raising campaign to build a new classroom building, a new library, and an addition to the science building and to convert the old library into administration offices. Under the auspices of the Little Rock University board of trustees, Richard C. Butler, president of the Com-

mercial National Bank, served as chairman of the drive, while James H. Penick, Sr., of the Worthen Bank and Trust Company, acted as vice-chairman. The campaign committee opened an office in the Tower Building in downtown Little Rock under the name of the Little Rock University Development Program and launched what board member Gus Ottenheimer called "the most challenging and stimulating effort of its kind the University has made since it was founded."[5] Under Butler's leadership, four division chairmen — Robert E. Ritchie (Pattern Gifts), R.A. Lile (Special Gifts), Houston J. Burford (Community Gifts), and Carey Stabler (University Division) — solicited funding for the college's physical expansion. Although Stabler later referred to these money-raising activities as "organized begging,"[6] the school's president recognized their importance for the survival of a private institution like LRU. He also acknowledged that generating revenue for the university had to be a continuous effort beyond the $1.5 million campaign. Consequently, Stabler established an Office of Development in the spring of 1964 and hired Neyland Hester, a former Methodist minister and instructor at Southern Methodist University in Dallas, to direct the school's development efforts. Over the remainder of the decade, Hester created a modern development program and headed all of Little Rock University's public relations as the institution launched an unprecedented era of growth.

Hester, Butler, Penick, and other leaders of the $1.5 million drive appealed to businesses and individual citizens in the greater Little Rock area to support their local college in order to attract new industry to the community and to keep capable students in central Arkansas. The *Arkansas Democrat* and the *Arkansas Gazette* urged their readers to contribute to the drive, and the *North Little Rock Times* played an active role in recruiting support for LRU in the northern part of Pulaski County. The *Times* ran editorials pointing out that 353 of LRU's 2100 students lived in North Little Rock and that 24 percent of the school's enrollment came from areas north of the Arkansas River. In addition, the paper echoed a theme included in every fundraising drive conducted by the school since its days as a junior college: "for many LRU represents their only chance to get a degree ... one final opportunity to finish the college education that was started in the past but had to be dropped for one reason or another."[7]

Solicitations for the campaign proceeded slowly, but by October 1964 the drive had raised over a million dollars. Eventually the efforts of the committee yielded over $1,300,000 and, combined with a series of federal grants and loans, provided the money to build the needed structures. On May 14, 1967, Little Rock University officials hosted dedication ceremonies for the new library and the new classroom building with Arkansas governor Winthrop Rockefeller delivering the principal address. Even with the facilities made possible by the $1.5 million campaign, however, school authorities recognized that further expansion of the college would be necessary to meet increasing enrollments and consequently viewed the new buildings not as a solution to the problems of overcrowding, but rather as the beginning of a construction boom at LRU that would extend into the next decade.

In 1965 university supporters launched a new $4.5 million physical expansion program that eventually resulted in an addition to the library, a physical education building, an annex to the student union, and a new power distribution system. In the late 1960s, the wooded acreage that had constituted Raymond Rebsamen's gift almost 20 years before evolved into a modern college complex. Understandably, this rapid transformation generated some confusion. Basements leaked, pipes burst, and aesthetic critics claimed some of the new edifices looked more suitable for a prison than a college. At one point the campus had nine restrooms marked "Ladies" and five marked "Women"; "Men" had a choice of five restrooms while "Gentlemen" had only four.[8] Naming buildings also posed a problem for the administration and the board of trustees. While other institutions of higher education acknowledged benefactors, ex-presidents, and distinguished professors by naming structures in their honor, Little Rock University's *Bulletin* for 1968 through 1970 listed the campus buildings under unimaginative titles like the New Library (not the Larson Memorial Library), the North Building, the South Building, the East Building, the Science Building, the Field House, the Student Union Building, and the Administration Building.

Although this situation improved following the merger with the University of Arkansas in 1969, when school officials named the East Building in honor of President Carey Stabler and the new library in honor of trustee Gus Ottenheimer, many pioneers in the development of the institution like George Donaghey and Raymond Rebsamen

*Commuters' problems. (1967 **Trojan,** 57)*

went unrecognized in this regard.

The construction boom at Little Rock University in the 1960s coincided with President John F. Kennedy's New Frontier and President Lyndon B. Johnson's Great Society programs — an era that constituted a high point in the history of federal aid to education — and, under Carey Stabler's leadership, LRU enjoyed an unprecedented bonanza of federal assistance in the expansion of the campus. In 1960 the institution received a $6500 grant from the Atomic Energy Commission as a result of a joint proposal submitted by LRU's physics and chemistry departments. In January 1961 the administration reached an agreement with the federal government to provide funds for counseling services for 25 counselees per month. Such initial efforts proved to be the beginning of a growing partnership between the government and the college. In the fall of 1964 President Stabler attended a historic gathering of the American Council on Education in San Francisco during which, according to Stabler, the "idea of welcoming the federal government as a desirable and reasonable partner in higher education was advocated strongly and warmly accepted by the entire conference."[9] After the meeting, he and other Little Rock University officials unhesitatingly pursued federal grants, loans, and subsidies to aid in the development of the institution.

LRU had participated in the National Defense Student Loan Program for several years, and by 1964 the college had $15,975 from the government available for student aid. Only three years later, in 1967, Little Rock University had an annual allotment of $88,000 through the same agency[10] and under the federally funded Work Study Program received over $63,000 a year to employ needy students who worked for $1.25 an hour. By 1966, the growing number of federal loans, grants, work programs, and scholarships plus similar programs funded through private means prompted the administration to appoint a student aid secretary — Jean Holmes — whose sole responsibilty involved coordinating these programs and handling applications for federal subsidies on the LRU campus.

The leadership of the college also relied heavily on Washington to finance the construction of the new buildings. Between the local campaigns for funds and the aid of the government, President Stabler later recalled that "of the two, the federal government was probably more than our own funds."[11] Little Rock University received a $166,654 federal Department of Health, Education, and Welfare grant for the construction of the library and a $770,000 loan from HEW to assist in building the classroom-theater building. However, it was denied a government loan to construct a nine-story coed dormitory to house 125 women and 100 men.[12]

During Carey Stabler's tenure as president, his job increasingly demanded that he travel to Washington, D.C., to meet with federal bureaucrats who controlled the disbursal of grants, loans, and other forms of aid. The board of trustees hired Carthal M. Harper as a special assistant to the president in charge of obtaining federal programs for the school. Through the efforts of Harper, Stabler, Hester, and other LRU officials, the college acquired grants for the library, federal help for the training of teacher aids, loans to subsidize the introduction of computers on the campus, and loans for the college's Allied Health Program to assist in the education of student nurses. The availability of extensive federal aid changed the nature of college administrations throughout the country in the 1960s. Administrators with primarily academic backgrounds had to learn the techniques of writing grant proposals and meeting with Washington authorities to insure that their institution received maximum federal assistance. By 1969, college administration had moved far beyond the days when John Larson served in the dual role of high school principal and Jaycee president.

Although federal assistance proved invaluable, community and corporate support remained an essential factor in LRU's development during this period, and to recruit that aid the governance structure of the college underwent a change in 1965. In January of that year, the Little Rock University Foundation transferred the title of the LRU campus to the school's board of trustees and consequently ceased to exist. The trustees already owned the student union building, and the addition of the remainder of the campus gave LRU a unified physical plant worth over $6 million. Since the Little Rock University Foundation had been organized to avoid any possible conflict of interest with the Little Rock School Board, the creation of a separate board of trustees in 1959 removed the need for the foundation. After 1965 all fund-raising drives were conducted directly under the authority of the Little Rock University board of trustees.[13]

During the revenue-raising campaigns of the 1960s, the major gifts came from local corporations, while national compa-

nies like Teletype, Gulf Oil, U.S. Steel, and Texaco made smaller grants for various purposes. In addition, several individual citizens in the greater Little Rock area continued to support the college. In 1965, Frederick Isaac (Ike) Beyer, a Little Rock insurance executive, willed $40,000 to the college, while a year later Mrs. Stella Boyle Smith donated $10,000 to establish an endowment fund for the music department. Future governor Winthrop Rockefeller made a $50,000 contribution to LRU in 1965 and donated smaller amounts on other occasions. Despite this generosity, school officials always believed Rockefeller should have played a more significant role in supporting Little Rock University. President Stabler later recalled serious discussions with board members about naming the school in Rockefeller's honor if the multi-millionaire would make a major contribution to the university, but commented that "when it came to LRU I'd say that the Rockefellers were not committed to us ...."[14]

A more significant commitment to LRU came from the family of Dr. W.G. Cooper, a former school board director, trustee, and longtime supporter of the college. Several members of Cooper's family donated $250,000 to the endowment fund in 1965 to honor Cooper and to "dramatize LRU's meteoric rise from a one-room junior college to a $6 to $8 million university." School officials used income from the gift to endow a chair of English and construct a decorative water fountain in front of the student union building. The donation also altered the institution's policy on awarding honorary degrees. In 1962 the board of trustees unanimously voted that LRU should not award honorary degrees, but five years later the membership awarded the college's first such degrees to Alfred Kahn, Sr., a patron of the school, and George F. Jewett, Jr., of California, a vice-president of Potlatch Forests, Incorporated, and a member of Cooper's family.[15]

LRU also continued to receive an annual allotment from the Donaghey Foundation. The foundation's board expanded the holdings of the original trust in the 1960s by purchasing six lots in the block bounded by Main, Louisiana, West Eighth, and West Ninth Streets in downtown Little Rock, raising the assets of the trust to over $5 million. Although the Donaghey Foundation contributed approximately $90,000 a year to LRU, by the late 1960s the college's survival did not depend as heavily on money from the Donaghey trust as it had a decade earlier because of federal assistance and community support.

Along with a bigger financial base, LRU's academic programs grew under the direction of an expanded faculty. One emblematic change in instructional personnel was the retirement in 1964 of Pauline Hoeltzel, the last of the original Little Rock Junior College faculty. Two years later Elmer Stahlkopf stepped down after 36 years of service to the institution. In 1967 Neyland Hester became an assistant to the president and Francis L. Robinson assumed the position of vice-president for finance. That same year Norman A. Baxter, a Harvard University graduate and protégé of President Stabler, completed his first full year as vice-president for academic affairs. Two years later Baxter left the university and James H. Fribourgh,

chairman of the Division of Biological Sciences, became vice-president for academic affairs. Margaret Moser served as acting librarian until 1965, when the administration hired James A. Allen, a former high school teacher and librarian at Louisiana State University, to head the LRU library. Allen directed the fortunes of the Little Rock University and University of Arkansas at Little Rock library for over 20 years, guiding the facility through several internal controversies.

During the late 1960s, the teaching staff at the college gained many new faculty members who were to play leading roles in the school's development over the ensuing decades. Dr. Ralph D. Eberly, a former professor of English at North Texas State University, filled LRU's first endowed chair — the William Grant Cooper, Jr., Chair of English — in 1967. Other instructors who joined the teaching staff included Roy D. Smith in accounting in 1963; Francis R. Ross in history in 1963; Mary Katherine Hardie in sociology in 1964; and David L. Wood in psychology in 1965. Through the efforts of President Stabler and the trustees, teachers' salaries at LRU in the late 1960s equaled, and instructors' salaries surpassed, the national average.[16] In addition, by September 1968 the administration had reduced teaching assignments from fifteen to twelve hours each semester, despite the fact that the smaller loads led to an increase in the number of students in each class. Part-time faculty members were replaced by full-time instructors, and by 1969, in a total instructional staff of 80, full-time teachers outnumbered part-time instructors for the first time since the institution became a senior college.[17]

The new teachers promoted innova-

Dr. James H. Fribourgh, professor of biology, chairman of the Division of Biological Science, and Vice-President for Academic Affairs. (1972 **Trojan,** *26)*

tive programs, introduced new courses, and sponsored academic activities outside their normal classroom duties. For example, Bedford Hadley of LRU's history department served as chairman of the arrangements committee for the annual meeting of the Southern Historical Association in Little Rock in 1964. Members of the English department sponsored the "Forum of Ideas," a lecture series begun in 1965 that brought outstanding speakers to the campus, including Dr. Wilfred Desan of Georgetown University, one of the nation's foremost experts on the works of existentialist writer Jean Paul Sartre.

Under the direction of the instructional staff, the number of courses offered by the college expanded from 81 in 1956 to over 500 by 1967. The addition of these courses represented a broadening of the educational opportunities provided by LRU beyond the basic arts and sciences curriculum. The Division of Biological Sciences, for instance, included a variety of offerings in preprofessional areas of applied biology like medicine, dentistry, nursing, pharmacy, dental hygiene, forestry, and wildlife management. School officials also instituted a program of lower-level courses at the Little Rock Air Force Base in 1965 that included all requirements for a bachelor's degree in business management.[18] By 1969 the curriculum had expanded to include a cooperative venture with the Baptist Memorial Hospital in Memphis for a degree in medical record science; a program in forestry in cooperation with Duke University in Durham, North Carolina; and a similar offering with the Mayo Clinic leading to a degree in physical therapy.[19] The administration leased an IBM 1130 in the fall of 1968 and hired

Philip Orahood as director and programmer of a computer science program. The majority of LRU students continued to major in these more practical areas of the curriculum, as evidenced by the fact that by 1967 the Division of Business and Economics ranked first in the university in terms of student enrollment. The growing number of business students, however, undercut the traditional liberal arts base of the curriculum, since university requirements exempted students majoring in accounting, business administration, management, and marketing from all but nineteen hours of basic general education courses in English, history, speech, and physical education.[20]

Some critics saw the growing number of business students as an indication that Little Rock University attracted less than the most capable undergraduates. In 1953 one concerned individual had written to a member of the school's board of trustees, "JC has never been defined as a fine and important institution of higher learning,"[21] and by the late 1950s, the school had achieved an unfair reputation in some quarters as what one campus editor called "a catchall for rejects from other colleges."[22] Even LRU students sometimes referred to their school as "Pine Cone U" or "Pine Tree Tech." The editor of the 1964 *Forum* wrote that "to some students, going to LRU is some type of undesirable punishment imposed upon them by their parents. To some this institution is the last chance college."[23] Students and others often joked that the initials LRU stood for "Last Resort University."

Part of this unfavorable image stemmed from the administration's

*Dr. Bedford K. Hadley, professor of history and chairman of the Division of Social Science. (1966 **Trojan**)*

choice of selective retention of students over selective admission. Under this policy the college admitted virtually everyone who applied and then dismissed those who could not make satisfactory academic progress. The *Bulletin* of 1957-58 stated that to enter LRU "applicants must furnish evidence of good moral character" (authorities omitted this qualification from subsequent bulletins) and listed a minimum of credits that would earn the student seeking admittance a high school diploma. By 1960, admission to LRU depended on the "personal and academic records of the applicant" and required that a prospective student be in the upper 80 percent of his high school graduating class.[24] This essentially open-admission policy remained unchanged throughout the 1960s and by 1966 the *Bulletin* included an acknowledgment that, in terms of entering Little Rock University, "many high school graduates with low scholastic records and test scores are entitled to an opportunity to seek a college education."[25] Several years after his retirement, former LRU president Carey Stabler recalled that his biggest disappointments as the head of the school came as a result of LRU's academic image. "I guess the least satisfaction I got," he told an interviewer, "was that we never came anywhere near establishing ourselves as an academically exclusive college."[26]

To increase enrollment and to try to improve the quality of the LRU student body, school officials conducted an aggressive recruiting campaign in the early 1960s. Efforts to convince high school students to attend the college, however, proved less than satisfactory. In 1961 Tom Broce, Little Rock University's chief

recruiter, informed President Stabler that the "college day" programs conducted by many Arkansas high schools "are not worth the gasoline it takes to drive to them."[27] Broce felt that Little Rock University lacked contacts among high school principals and accused several academic departments and the registrar's office at LRU with being uncooperative in recruiting efforts.[28] The administration held several conferences on the matter, but faculty members found most ideas for attracting students distasteful. One administrator recommended that to recruit new undergraduates, "we must provide them with forms of entertainment, such as football, dormitories, and national fraternities,"[29] and other suggestions which the instructional staff dismissed included "an easing of tough grade distribution in certain departments, especially in freshmen level courses."[30]

Still, the students who attended Little Rock University represented a cross-section of academic ability and motivation. Even though by 1967 almost one-third of the LRU student body had lower than a C average,[31] basic test scores indicated that the average LRU undergraduate ranked in the upper quarter of all students in the state and in the upper half of students throughout the nation.[32] Despite the recruitment problems it was clear that, far from being a university of last resort, LRU attracted some individuals who could have done well at any college in the country, along with others whose lack of motivation or skills prevented them from achieving success in their college work.

Little Rock University tried to recognize and reward its successful students. In 1966 the institution established the

Edward Lynn Whitbeck Award — a $200 savings bond given to a qualified senior. A gift from Mr. and Mrs. Frank Whitbeck in memory of their son, who died shortly before his graduation from LRU, the award included a bronze plaque. Over the years the recipients represented some of the finest students in the school's history.[33]

In addition to the many outstanding undergraduates who distinguished themselves during their collegiate days, numerous graduates of LRU achieved success and gained honors in a variety of fields both in Arkansas and outside the state. While those individuals may have attended Little Rock University for a variety of reasons, the skills and knowledge they acquired there aided them in later endeavors. Alumni or people who began their studies during the LRU era included Judges Judith Rogers and Joyce Warren; associate director of the Federal Bureau of Investigation William Lee Colwell; Arkansas Power and Light Company president Jerry Maulden; and First Commercial Bank vice president Charles Stewart. In 1966, LRU student body president Jerry Rose won the first Fulbright Scholarship given to a Little Rock University student, which he used to study political science in New Zealand.[34] A year later Robert Palmer, a recent LRU graduate, journeyed to New York City, where he became one of the most respected music critics in the country. Writing for the *New York Times*, *Rolling Stone* magazine, the *Atlantic Monthly*, and other journals, Palmer became a major voice in the development of American popular music over the ensuing 20 years. He also wrote several books, including *Delta Blues*, an examination of the musical traditions found in rural areas of the Mississippi River basin.[35]

Because a high percentage of Little Rock University students lived at home with their parents or spouse and because many students had to work their way through school, the student body at Little Rock University tended to be more preoccupied with their day-to-day lives than with the issues surrounding the wave of radicalism that rocked the nation's campuses in the late 1960s. However, a small group of LRU students felt that questions like American involvement in Vietnam, equal rights for black citizens, and a system of higher education that depersonalized those who wanted to learn, merited active involvement. The LRU chapter of the Wesley Foundation, the Methodist ministry to college students, provided an early stimulus to local undergraduates concerned with social issues. Operating out of a building at 32nd and Taylor Streets near the campus, the Wesley Foundation established a series of coffeehouses in the mid-1960s that attracted students and other interested citizens. The Inn of the Fishermen at the corner of Fourth and Elm served apple cider, coffee, and sandwiches and featured popular folk singing groups like the Solip Singers, who performed musical numbers by social critics like Bob Dylan and Dick and Mimi Farina. In 1966 "Dante's Inferno" provided similar activities at the Wesley Foundation building, and in 1967 the coffeehouse became "The Exit," a name intended as a retort to Sartre's play "No Exit." Black and white students as well as nonstudents gathered at The Exit to play records, strum guitars, sing, and discuss the state of modern society. Despite the harmless nature of the coffeehouses, the Wesley Foundation became a suspected haven of radicalism and fell under the close scrutiny of the LRU administration. In May 1967, Dean of Men Jerry D. Corley informed officials of the local Methodist Church that the activities of the Wesley Foundation "reflect negatively on the image of LRU." Corley further suggested that the governing board of the church launch an investigation of the local Methodist student club.[36]

Corley got his wish. During the summer of 1967, a committee of ministers and lay leaders initiated an investigation of the Methodist campus organization and the group's director, the Reverend Harold J. Wells. Wells contended the church hierarchy's unhappiness with his program stemmed from his open opposition to the war in Vietnam. One minister on the examining committee confirmed the frivolous nature of the undertaking when he responded to a question about what was wrong with the Wesley Foundation by saying, "There are quite a few people hanging around there who look like they need to go to the barber shop and the laundry."[37] Although the committee failed to find any evidence of radical activity or misconduct, Reverend Wells accepted a new position with the church in Iowa in 1968.

Wells, whom some members of the LRU administration blamed for radicalizing local students, left a campus that in fact did reflect some concern with issues like Vietnam. In February 1966 over 300 people attended a "teach-in" on Vietnam sponsored by LRU's Foreign Relations Council. That same month an unofficial campus group called LRU Students Concerned about the War in Vietnam staged a march through Mac-

Arthur Park in a drizzling Saturday afternoon rain. The demonstration was the first of its kind in Arkansas, and the conservative Student Senate at the college disavowed the protest in a meek resolution that questioned idealism and favored realism in U.S. foreign policy.[38] Almost three years after the demonstration in the park, over 1000 people wearing either black or red, white, and blue armbands filled the student union building for a debate on the war between representatives of the Progressive Democrats and Young Americans for Freedom.[39]

The Vietnam War also provided the subject for numerous articles in the *Forum*. Its editors also criticized hate groups like the Capital Citizens Council of Little Rock, editorialized against a police raid of an interracial party in the city's Granite Mountain area, and endorsed state and local political candidates. This willingness to print stories about social and political issues marked a change from the more conservative campus paper of the 1950s, and though some students and faculty members applauded the new journalism, the administration found the *Forum* of the late 1960s to be a source of embarrassment. In the spring of 1967, President Stabler reported to the board of trustees that he had received numerous complaints about the *Forum* and proposed that his office either close down the paper because "it fills no great need or purpose" or at least censor it.[40] The board, however, took a more tolerant view and refused to endorse such repressive measures, clearing the way for the paper to remain a campus institution for many years.

A small group of LRU students took

Voting in a student election in the 1960s (UALR News Bureau Photos '67/'68, Roll B)

up the nationwide concern with a depersonalized system of higher education. One campus group circulated literature asking, "Are you one of the cavalcaded students who are aware of the oligaric [sic] conditions at LRU, but are afraid to react constructively because of its unjust consequences?"[41] Such expressions made President Stabler overreact to the possibility of student militancy. At one point he promised the advisory council that he was prepared to resort to "full police power" if students got out of hand. Fortunately he never had to take such action, because most students confined their concerns about the school to requests for reasonable alterations in its operations — petitioning for measures like a full week of Easter holidays, improved drainage around the campus, lower cafeteria prices, and extended library hours, to which the administration responded positively by initiating the suggested changes.

College officials also reacted positively to student concerns over the treatment of black undergraduates. During the 1968-69 school year an unofficial campus organization called Students for Equality presented a list of grievances to the LRU Student Senate that used the harsh rhetoric so often employed during the era. "The Blacks of Little Rock University," the preface to the petition read, "have been denied the use of their influence and their talents through a school system which stifles initiative, discourages the newcomer, and crushes the hopeful...."[42] Under the leadership of its president David Wilmot-Freedman, the group requested that among other things the administration offer a black humanities course, hire black faculty members, form black social groups, and

eliminate faculty prejudices toward black students.

Almost immediately the administration resolved to "enthusiastically recruit and hire black faculty members,"[43] and in the fall of 1969 the school's curriculum included a course entitled "Readings in Negro History and Literature," for which 25 students including 9 blacks enrolled. According to President Stabler the large registration for the course "was a good deal more than we expected." Wilmot-Freedman criticized the course as being "tokenism."[44] Despite such comments, the faculty and administration of Little Rock University responded with sensitivity to the needs of the black students who attended the institution. Along with recruiting black instructors and offering the humanities course, school authorities also officially recognized the SFE; supported Alpha Phi Alpha, a racially integrated fraternity; and increased the number of black senior counselors. Through these efforts the college avoided much of the racial tension that marked other campuses throughout the country in the late 1960s.

While a small percentage of LRU students actively opposed racism or the Vietnam War, the vast majority spent their college years in the same basic pattern that had characterized campus life since the founding of the institution in 1927. Although by the late 1960s Stunt Night, the All-School Picnic, and Donaghey Day no longer highlighted the social calendar, new activites like Aulsing — a festival where campus organizations competed against each other in singing Christmas songs — provided the same type of school-sponsored entertainment. New Greek groups like Pi Kappa Alpha for men and Chi Omega for wom-

*The campus "Aulsing" festival. (1965 **Trojan,** 75).*

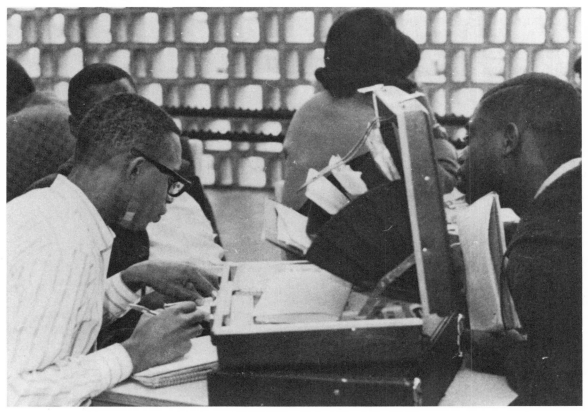

*Studying in the student union building between classes. (1968 **Trojan)***

en became a part of campus life in 1964, and "The Levee" on South University, which featured the music of folk-singing groups like the Rivermen along with beer and pizza, became a popular hangout for LRU students, both Greek and non-Greek. Most Little Rock University students, however, filled their days with classes, part-time jobs, and studying and found little extra time for either parties or protests.

These students forged Little Rock University's identity in the 1960s — a private commuter college offering basic educational opportunities to students of all ages in the greater Little Rock area. Beginning in the middle years of the decade, though, a movement that would dramatically alter that identity began to gain momentum, as articles, stories, and talk about a merger between Little Rock University and the University of Arkansas at Fayetteville started to circulate through the community.

*Welcoming ceremonies for new fraternity pledges in 1965. (1966 **Trojan**)*

C H A P T E R   T W E L V E

Merger

A shadow hovered over campus life at LRU in the late 1960s. Whether students gathered for fraternity parties, basketball games, or an evening at The Exit, their conversation often reflected undercurrents of doubt about the future of their school. The students' concern stemmed from reports that a merger of Little Rock University and the University of Arkansas at Fayetteville would soon convert the capital city's small, private college into a sprawling state university.

On the surface, campus activities proceeded in a normal fashion. Students registered for classes in a process one undergraduate said transformed the Student Union into "a jungle of clawing, screaming students determined not to be stuck with dawn-to-dusk classes."[1] Instructors held classes as usual, clubs met, social groups had parties, intramural teams competed. A coin-operated copier in the library in 1964 revolutionized the processes of note-taking. The *Forum* became a weekly paper for the first time in 1967. Students continued to gather in the Union between classes, study in the library, and leave campus to go to work as usual. Beneath that steady rhythm of college existence, however, anxiety about what many Little Rock students called a "take-

over" by the University of Arkansas characterized life at LRU.

Some critics blamed the decline of varsity athletics at the school on the uncertain conditions generated by talk of a merger. Dr. James Fribrough, the academic vice-president of LRU in 1969, later recalled that during that era "the merger took so much time and energy there was no time for athletics or other activities."[2] In 1962 the administration, acting on a recommendation by the faculty, reinstituted tennis, baseball, and golf, although with the exception of golf, none of the teams achieved much recognition or support from school authorities by the end of the decade.

When head basketball coach Bill Ballard resigned in 1965, the administration replaced him with Cleve Branscum, Ballard's assistant and a 1963 graduate of the school. Two years later Branscum also resigned. Dr. James R. Hall became athletic director and helped select Happy Mahfouz, a coach at Catholic High School in Little Rock, to head LRU's basketball program. While most Arkansas colleges awarded fifteen to twenty scholarships for basketball players, the administration reduced the school's allotment to ten and refused to allow outside sources to donate additional money for scholarships.[3] By 1968 the Trojan bas-

Trojan baseball — part of the LRU administration's effort to offer a complete varsity sports program in the late 1960s. (UALR News Bureau Photos '69/'70, Roll M)

ketball team, because of poor grades, injuries, and lack of interest, consisted of only six players. Hopes for a revived sports program at LRU that had arisen at the beginning of the decade evaporated as the administration and the board of trustees devoted an increasing amount of time and effort to the proposed merger with the Fayetteville school.

Almost 100 years before, the University of Arkansas had evolved from the Morrill Act — the measure passed by Congress in 1862 that established colleges to teach agriculture and the mechanical arts. The Civil War delayed the implementation of the bill in Arkansas until 1872, when the Arkansas Industrial University opened in Fayetteville with 321 students under the presidency of Noah P. Gates. Since the Morrill Act provided that any county or community might bid for the location of the college, a group of leading Little Rock citizens had earlier advocated a bond issue of $200,000 to bring the school to the capital city. Pulaski County voters, however, overwhelmingly rejected the bond issue, and bids by Batesville and Prairie Grove were considerably lower than the $100,000 bond issue passed by the citizens of Washington County and the $30,000 in city bonds offered by Fayetteville. Thus authorities selected the northwest Arkansas site for the state university.[4]

Renamed the University of Arkansas in 1899, the college reached an enrollment of 800 by 1913 and grew to over 3000 by 1930. Long known for fielding quality football squads, the university acquired the nickname "Razorbacks" in 1909, when Coach Hugo Bezdek referred to his team as "a wild band of Razor-back hogs."[5] On the eve of World War I officials at the Fayetteville campus added a college of education and in the 1920s a school of law and a graduate school. In the late 1940s the University of Arkansas became one of the first major state universities in the South to admit black students.

In 1957 school authorities opened a modern University of Arkansas Medical Center in Little Rock. They had operated a medical school in Pulaski County for many years, but the decision to expand it was an important sign of university officials' interest in strengthening the U. of A. presence in the capital city. In 1957 state legislators also authorized the establishment of the university's Graduate Institute of Technology in Pulaski County, to provide graduate resident instruction and research opportunities in the physical sciences, engineering, and mathematics.

A few years earlier, when LRJC was in the process of becoming a four-year school, it had come close to uniting with the U. of A. In 1955 the Ottenheimer Committee — the citizens' group conducting the comprehensive survey leading to Jaycee's expansion — had advocated that any senior college in Little Rock become an adjunct to the University of Arkansas. The committee's second recommendation was a school supported solely by local taxes. Ironically, its last preference was a private institution; the Ottenheimer Report stated that "it is doubtful that the program of a private college could be expanded sufficiently to meet the needs of the community."[6]

The members of the LRJC faculty, however, wanted an independent college and opposed any affiliation with the University of Arkansas. In part this

*Dr. David W. Mullins, president of the University of Arkansas at the time of its merger with Little Rock University in 1969. (1972 **Trojan)***

attitude resulted from the likelihood that in view of several rulings by the United States Supreme Court, if the Little Rock school were to receive financial support from the state, black students could not be banned from campus.[7] According to Harold Engstrom, a long-time trustee of the Little Rock school, U. of A. officials wanted to absorb the college that became LRU and, in fact, "agreement [to merge] was reached in 1957, but implementation was frustrated by the Little Rock integration crisis.[8]

In 1960, after the failed effort to combine the two institutions, David Wiley Mullins, a University of Arkansas graduate and former executive vice-president of Auburn University in Alabama, became president of the U. of A. The early years of his administration featured considerable physical expansion on the Fayetteville campus, but during the late 1960s Mullins devoted his efforts to making a merger between his school and Little Rock University a reality. By that time hostility toward uniting the institutions had subsided in the capital city, and under Mullins's leadership impulses for a merger began gaining momentum.

One factor favoring a change was the inability of Little Rock University to establish the graduate programs that were in growing demand in central Arkansas. Initially school officials hoped to offer graduate courses fairly soon. In 1964, in response to inquiries from public school authorities and teachers in the city who hoped the local college could someday provide master's programs in education, the LRU board of trustees approved a study of the feasibility of establishing a graduate school on the campus. After investigating the matter, the LRU faculty expressed optimism that the school might be able to offer a master's in business education, a master's in business administration, and a master of arts in teaching degree in the near future.[9]

However, officials from the North Central Association felt the college had to improve in several areas in order to offer quality graduate work. They recommended a 100-percent increase in the number of doctorates among the faculty and suggested that the library — which then had only about 50,000 books — needed more than twice that many to support master's-level courses. In 1966 Karl H. Dannenfeldt, a consultant from the North Central Association who reported on LRU, stressed the high cost of graduate education and warned that at that time the school's facilities appeared inadequate to support expansion into master's level programs.[10]

Yet the need for locally available graduate education intensified. Not only teachers in the area, but other college graduates who wanted to remain in Little Rock, sought advanced study. In addition, in the early part of the decade, the federal Atomic Energy Commission considered locating a multimillion-dollar nuclear accelerator in Pulaski County, but dropped the idea because the facility needed to be near a strong research-oriented university.[11] The AEC rejection of Little Rock was a keen reminder that the community suffered from its lack of graduate education, and consequently spurred officials at the University of Arkansas to investigate the possibility of expanding their graduate programs into the central counties of the state.[12]

Another factor that proved conducive to a merger was Little Rock University's worsening financial situation. Although

Commencement Day. (UALR News Bureau Photos '67/'68, Roll N)

never in a real crisis, LRU suffered many of the same economic problems that plagued other private educational institutions in the late 1960s — spiralling tuition costs, competition from tax-supported institutions in recruiting competent faculty, and increasing difficulty in raising revenues from the private sector. By 1967, President Stabler informed his advisory council that operational budgets at LRU would have to be decreased by as much as 15 percent and in some cases 20 percent, despite recent rises in tuition. A year later, reporting the school's financial situation to be "the toughest it has been since I have been at LRU," Stabler requested an increase in the Donaghey Foundation's annual appropriation to the college from $90,000 to $125,000.[13] A study conducted by the board of trustees also showed that between 1967 and 1980 LRU would have to raise $18 million for capital improvements — a frightening prospect for a private school that had never raised anywhere near that much in the previous 40 years of its existence. The situation made one observer comment, "[A]s a privately financed institution LRU cannot meet the growing demands for higher education in the face of rising costs."[14] A Fayetteville professor later wrote that at LRU "finances steadily became more difficult … and stark economic reality compelled ultimate surrender [to the U. of A. merger]."[15]

Despite budgetary hardships, LRU rested on a solid reputation as a private four-year institution, and the initiative for merger came entirely from Fayetteville. U. of A. officials not only recognized the need for graduate work in the central counties of the state, but also wanted to revitalize their commitment to education in general. For their institution had problems of its own. "The U. of A. appears to be suffering from a lack of vitality," a *North Little Rock Times* editor wrote in 1966. "If it had not been for the increase in sheer numbers of students, the football team and several fights over academic freedom, the U. of A. would not have attracted much attention these past few years. Perhaps the opening of the central Arkansas campus would give it the shot in the arm it appears to need."[16]

The first step toward developing that facility came on June 29, 1965, when President Mullins of the university appointed an ad hoc committee to study the need for university programs and services in central Arkansas.[17] Headed by Storm Whaley, the vice-president for health sciences at the university, the committee relied on research conducted by Dr. Forrest Pollard of the Industrial Research and Extension Center, an expert in demographic studies of the state, and Dr. James L. Miller, Jr., the associate director for research of the Southern Regional Education Board, who served as an advisor to the committee on survey procedures. The Whaley Committee found that from 1950 to 1960, while Arkansas as a whole lost 6.5 percent population, central Arkansas gained 7.5 percent, and that from 1960 to 1964 the area's population increased from 566,019 to 616,533, or from 31.7 to 32.4 percent of the total population of the state.[18] These figures indicated that the availability of higher educational opportunities in the area was not commensurate with the increase in population. A genuine need existed for additional bachelor's and graduate level programs. After a year of study, the Whaley Com-

*Between classes. (1968 **Trojan**)*

mittee issued an interim report recommending that the University of Arkansas expand the school's graduate offerings in Little Rock and establish an undergraduate program in the central portion of the state to support the proposed graduate school. To accomplish these goals most efficiently, the committee further suggested that officials of the Fayetteville institution explore the possibility of merging with Little Rock University.[19]

As news of the Whaley Committee's findings reached the LRU community, many trustees, administrators, and faculty members responded with caution. In March 1966 President Stabler told the LRU board of trustees, "I regret to report that the [Whaley Committee] study … is developing into a plan for a major campus for a state institution of higher education in Little Rock."[20] The board, along with other LRU supporters, correctly perceived the prospect of the University of Arkansas's creating a branch campus in the capital city as a direct threat to the survival of Little Rock University.[21] Since tuition at state schools equaled about a third of the tuition at LRU, clearly students in the area would be inclined to abandon the private college and attend a local tax-supported university.

Initially, Stabler and the LRU board of trustees were undecided about how to respond to the overtures from Fayetteville. The majority of the board preferred that their college oppose any proposal which would compromise LRU's independent and private status, but a few members foresaw the possibility of LRU's becoming a state college to support the forthcoming University of Arkansas graduate programs in Little Rock. The president of LRU, however,

at first resisted the idea of a merger. In a later interview Stabler said, "[M]y aspiration and ambition was to build an outstanding private university,"[22] although he also indicated that he changed his mind following a meeting with President Mullins and other university leaders at a hotel in Little Rock.[23]

To resolve the situation, in July 1966 the LRU board of trustees agreed to cooperate with the University of Arkansas board in forming a fourteen-member committee to explore any merger possibilities. Under the leadership of LRU trustee chairman Penick and Dallas P. Raney, his counterpart from the university, the committee examined the salaries, faculties, curricula, and endowments of the two institutions in the hope of finding an acceptable method of providing additional higher education in central Arkansas. The committee's negotiations moved slowly, and by the fall President Stabler commented that over the past few months LRU had suffered seriously from the "merger malady."[24]

Part of his impatience stemmed from the adverse reaction by LRU students to reports of the proposed merger. In September 1966 the LRU *Forum* reported that in the previous year, 40 instructors had resigned from the university staff for reasons varying from lack of academic freedom to low salaries and quoted a former Fayetteville professor who claimed that the individuals connected with the University of Arkansas were overly concerned with the school's image and approached every problem of academic freedom from a public relations stance. The paper pointed out that the university remained on the censure list of the American Association of University Professors and questioned

Registration at LRU in the late 1960s. (UALR News Bureau Photos '66/'67, Roll B)

whether Little Rock University would receive any scholastic advantage from a merger with the Fayetteville school, saying that "the entire proposal looks like a step down for LRU."[25]

Seniors at LRU raised the point that if the merger succeeded they would hold a degree from a defunct college. In rhetoric typical of the 1960s, some LRU students also voiced concern that officials had failed to solicit any student opinions on the matter and challenged the "multiversity" concept, which they argued alienated students and teachers and led to the kind of impersonal educational system that could result in riots like those at the University of California at Berkeley a few years before. By October, letters to the editor objecting to the merger flooded the *Forum* office. "A spectre is haunting the campus," one student wrote. "The spectre of merger. We would become a political football for Arkansas politicans. State funds are accompanied by state control."[26]

No one in authority really cared what the LRU students thought, and negotiations to combine the two universities continued. President Mullins of the University of Arkansas promoted the idea in speeches across the state. In an address to the Little Rock Rotary Club he stressed that a merger would be "the most expeditious and effective course in moving to meet the total higher educational needs of central Arkansas." In that same speech the University of Arkansas president spoke in terms of a "University of Arkansas at Little Rock," although he added that such an institution would in no way weaken the main campus at Fayetteville. Mullins further informed the Rotarians that similar mergers had become a well-established

pattern in neighboring states like Missouri and Louisiana.[27]

Whatever optimism Mullins had for the merger of the two schools dissipated by December 1966. The ongoing negotiations between the two boards reached a stalemate before Christmas, and Penick told the press "there is no immediate possibility of a merger with Little Rock University and the University of Arkansas."[28] The major problem at this juncture involved the LRU trustees' desire to maintain considerable autonomy in any consolidation effort. This stance proved virtually impossible since the state constitution provided for a governing board to oversee the University of Arkansas that consisted of ten members selected on a largely geographic basis. Constitutionally, the University of Arkansas board could not be increased and the trustees could not delegate authority to a subordinate board. Unable to overcome this obstacle, the talks reached an impasse by the end of the year, and in January 1967 President Stabler circulated a memorandum among LRU faculty, staff, and students stating that the lack of progress by the trustees in regard to the merger compelled him to consider Little Rock University's permanent status to be that of an independent, private institution.[29] The editor of the *Forum* mistakenly took Stabler's memorandum as the last word on the subject and editorialized that the "little guy" had thwarted the efforts of the leviathan and commented that "in the near future the Trojans won't be 'callin' the Hogs.'"[30]

Talks between representatives of the two universities continued, however, and by the spring of 1967 the prospects of a merger appeared considerably more likely than they had in the winter. The

Little Rock University faculty had initiated a new study of the need to expand the educational opportunities in central Arkansas. The instructional staff seemed positive that a merger might be the only way to meet the demand for graduate and other advanced programs in the area. In July 1967, after two years of prolonged study and negotiation, the boards of trustees of Little Rock University and the University of Arkansas agreed to merge their respective institutions, pending the approval of the state legislature.

According to the terms of the agreement, President Stabler of LRU would become chancellor of the newly created University of Arkansas at Little Rock; fees, tuition, and salaries would be the same at both campuses; a fifteen-member Board of Visitors would be established for the new school and allowed to appoint two members to sit with the University of Arkansas trustees at all board meetings. In addition, endowments and gifts given in the past to Little Rock University or Little Rock Junior College would remain with UALR. In a joint announcement, Dallas Raney of the University of Arkansas board and E. Grainger Williams of the LRU trustees emphasized that the members of both groups believed that combining the two institutions would be in the best interest of each university and the people of central Arkansas.

But opponents in other areas of Arkansas voiced severe criticism of the trustees' actions, arguing that such an extension of the University of Arkansas would harm other state colleges and concentrate too much power in the capital city. Spokesmen from Fayetteville, Conway, Jonesboro, Arkadelphia, and

Magnolia contended that a merger would mean that millions of dollars of tax money would go to the Little Rock campus instead of to colleges in their communities. The Hot Springs *Sentinel-Record* went to the heart of the opposition in a July 16, 1967, editorial which argued that a state-supported university in Little Rock would eventually become the main campus of the University of Arkansas, outstripping isolated Fayetteville in terms of enrollment, graduate programs, appropriations, and possibly even athletics. "This may be the whole idea," the Garland County paper said, "of those Little Rock interests who are fighting so hard to create a major threat to Arkansas's total system of higher education."[31]

Historically, the outlying areas of the state had always been suspicious of the capital city — sometimes with good reason. In the late 1920s, for example, a group of Little Rock citizens launched an attempt to relocate the entire University of Arkansas from Fayetteville to Pulaski County. The campaign not only failed but generated widespread antagonism toward the capital city, and leaders of the aborted drive journeyed to Fayetteville to give the local Chamber of Commerce a grandfather clock as a symbolic peace offering. Even at the time of the establishment of Little Rock Junior College in 1927, some University of Arkansas faculty members and citizens of Fayetteville complained that the creation of a two-year collegiate program in the middle of the state might reduce enrollment at the University of Arkansas.

This same kind of argument surfaced throughout the summer of 1967, as local leaders in several Arkansas communities mounted a campaign to prevent the proposed merger. State Senator Hugh Lookadoo of Arkadelphia warned that the new university in Little Rock would not only be a financial disaster but would damage the two schools in his hometown, Henderson State College and Ouachita Baptist University. Representative Cecil Alexander of Heber Springs condemned the merger as well, arguing that officials who wanted to create a strong university in central Arkansas should build on the foundation already established at the tax-supported State College of Arkansas in Conway. Representative J.C. Dawson echoed Alexander's position and pointed out what he regarded as the ultimate disaster of the merger by charging that if the plan succeeded, "Fayetteville would lose the Razorbacks to Little Rock."[32] Dawson's remark caused one pundit to observe that apparently people from all over Arkansas feared that the capital city, as usual, was trying to "hog" everything.

Supporters of the merger responded to these attacks by publicizing the fact that professional studies continually demonstrated that uniting the two institutions would be a realistic and financially sound way to serve the educational needs of the people of central Arkansas. In the fall of 1967, President Mullins of the Fayetteville campus and President Stabler of LRU joined Doug Brandon, a Pulaski County legislator, on a local television program advocating an immediate merger. The panelists contended that with the Graduate Institute of Technology and the medical school, the University of Arkansas was already established in the capital city, and the creation of a complete campus of the main university in Little Rock would provide thousands of students with an economical opportunity to participate in the benefits of higher education.

Other groups and individuals also voiced support for the plan. Dr. W.B. Stiles, director of the Graduate Institute of Technology, wrote a public letter arguing that additional members of a combined GIT and LRU instructional staff would not only be available to teach both undergraduate and graduate courses, but a stronger research-oriented faculty could help attract new "high-tech" industries to Pulaski County and build on the GIT's national reputation in fields like mass spectrometry and gas-phase chronomotography.[33] In November 1967 the University of Arkansas Alumni Association's board of directors joined the movement favoring consolidation of the two schools, unanimously endorsed the proposed merger, and urged Arkansas Governor Winthrop Rockefeller to move quickly on the matter.

Rockefeller, however, proceeded with caution. Despite pleas from President Stabler that LRU's fund-raising efforts had been damaged by the college's uncertain future and doubts that the institution could survive as a private college, the governor refused to include the merger in a special session of the Arkansas legislature scheduled to meet in January 1968. Rockefeller had publicly supported the idea, but cited a lack of funds to finance the merger as his chief reason for not placing the issue on the special session agenda. Both advocates and detractors of the plan began organizing for the regular legislative meeting the following year. In the meantime, LRU's enrollment reached a record 3100 students for the spring term in 1968, a fact that accentuated the need for expanded higher educational facilities

President Stabler meeting with students in the LRU student union building.
*(1969 **Trojan)***

for central Arkansas.

Despite growing momentum, later that same year, the Arkansas Commission on Coordination of Higher Educational Finance introduced a series of recommendations that jeopardized the proposed merger. Created in 1961, the ACCHEF included ten members from various parts of Arkansas whose main task involved unifying the work of the state's eight tax-supported colleges and universities by evaluating budget requests from all the schools and asking the legislature for a single allocation. Although the commission remained an advisory body with no legal authority, the ACCHEF represented statewide educational interests and exerted considerable influence on the governor's office. In regard to the pending merger, the commission submitted a plan under which LRU would become the University of Arkansas at Little Rock but would have a student body consisting of only juniors, seniors, and graduate students. At the same time, educational authorities would have to establish a separate community college in Pulaski County to serve freshmen and sophomores and the voters of central Arkansas would have to approve a tax millage for the construction and operation of the new two-year institution.

The leadership of LRU strongly opposed the concept, maintaining that under any reorganization, Little Rock University should remain a traditional four-year college. Although the University of Arkansas board of trustees took no stand on the commission's recommendations, President Mullins promised to appeal to the legislature to modify efforts to tie the merger to the creation of a community college. Governor Rocke-

feller, however, issued a compromise proposal in December 1968 that called for a four-year merged university in Little Rock contingent on Pulaski County's establishing a separate junior college. The *North Little Rock Times* accurately reflected the sentiment toward the matter in the capital city by calling the governor's idea "unrealistic and ridiculous," and, because of the confusion generated by the ACCHEF and the governor's suggested compromise, by the opening of the 1969 legislative session the fate of LRU remained in doubt.

This doubt was removed and the future of higher education in central Arkansas became much clearer during the meeting of the Arkansas General Assembly in January 1969. Through the united and determined efforts of the Pulaski County House and Senate delegations, the legislature passed Act 35 early in the session and, with the governor's signature on February 10, 1969, the measure became law. The act authorized the University of Arkansas board of trustees "to operate as a part thereof a campus to be known as 'the University of Arkansas at Little Rock' incorporating therein the private institution now known as Little Rock University."[34] The measure did not include a provision for a community college, and Rockefeller signed the bill with the assurance of civic leaders in central Arkansas that they would help establish a junior college in Pulaski County in the near future.

Led by Senator Ben Allen, the Pulaski County legislators (13 of 100 representatives and 5 of 35 senators) did not merge the two institutions without having to combat substantial opposition. State Senator Guy H. (Mutt) Jones of Conway outmaneuvered the senators from Pu-

A meeting of the board of trustees and the administration to plan the merger with the University of Arkansas in 1969. (1969
Trojan)

*Students study the college's long-range expansion plans in 1969. (1969 **Trojan**)*

Governor Winthrop Rockefeller signing the bill authorizing the merger of Little Rock University and the University of Arkansas at Fayetteville in 1969. (1969 **Trojan,** *24)*

iaski County on several occasions and temporarily delayed the passage of the bill. "I might not be able to stop this train," Jones said, "but I'm going to slow it down a little."[35] The Pulaski County delegation traded numerous votes to get the measure passed. At one point Senator Richard Earl Griffin of Crossett, a supporter of Jones, flung his copy of the Senate rules across the chamber and burst into tears over the prospect of locating an extension of the University of Arkansas in the capital city.[36]

Following the passage of the merger bill, the legislature passed an appropriations measure to fund the new institution through the state's Revenue Stabilization Act, which the General Assembly amended to include a separate fund for the University of Arkansas at Little Rock. Although the legislators approved expenditures of over $3 million in 1969-70 and $7 million the following year, because of the formula for the distribution of money under the act UALR received no money from the top "A" category of the Revenue Stabilization funds, and consequently received considerably less funding the first two years of operation as a state school than the administration anticipated. Even after the governor signed the merger bill, opposition to creating UALR continued. The Fayetteville Junior Chamber of Commerce attempted to call for a statewide referendum on Act 35 and Jaycee members from all over Arkansas circulated petitions in 30 counties to make the measure part of the next general election. Much to their surprise, they discovered a lack of enthusiasm on the part of the people of the state for any attempt to halt the merger, and the Jay-

cees finally abandoned the effort in June 1969.[37]

Later that summer, trustees of both universities executed a revised agreement making the merger of the two schools official as of September 1. At that time, several members of the LRU board reemphasized their belief that the union would not end LRU, but rather would perpetuate the institution under a new name, increasing the usefulness of the college founded over 40 years earlier in the local high school. Although at first board members Richard Butler and Hugh Patterson had favored maintaining LRU as a private university, by the time of the signing of the final document in July, the consensus of the trustees was that merger was the best way for the college to expand its mission and to avoid the financial and other difficulties facing private institutions throughout the country. According to the July agreement, President Stabler became the chancellor of the new university, and school officials lowered the $20 per semester-hour tuition at the Little Rock campus to $17 per semester-hour. Finally, the following spring, university authorities combined the commencement exercises for all University of Arkansas programs in Little Rock — UALR, GIT, and the medical school — as a symbol of the successful conclusion of the merger.

UALR received the school's first allotment of state funds in December 1969, officially marking the transition from a private institution to a tax-supported one, and that fall the University of Arkansas at Little Rock enrolled 3,527 students while the Fayetteville campus had 10,950. Administrative officials publicly maintained that the transition went as smoothly as possible, although some

*The Little Rock University campus in the spring of 1969. (1969 **Trojan**)*

resentment lingered long after the creation of the state school in Little Rock. Even before the completion of the merger, President Stabler wrote to a friend in Alabama that "after fifteen months of futile resistance we have agreed to a complete takeover by the U. of A., leaving our own Board of Trustees rather unimportant and probably insignificant."[38] Stabler feared his beloved campus would be swallowed by the larger Fayetteville institution, and after his retirement the former UALR chancellor confessed to one interviewer that as far as the attitude exhibited by officials from the University of Arkansas was concerned "they were everything and we were nothing."[39] The UALR faculty also shared some of Stabler's apprehension, and although they reluctantly supported the merger, several years later some instructors publicly questioned the wisdom of the decision.

Still, the combining of the two institutions held great potential for the advancement of higher education in the state, to the extent that one local newspaper editor called the merger "the most significant development in higher education in Arkansas."[40] By becoming the University of Arkansas at Little Rock, the school offered reduced tuition rates and expanded the college's programs to include needed graduate education and research facilities, thereby continuing the Little Rock campus's tradition of being a "people's college." In addition, the merger gave the Fayetteville-based University of Arkansas a vital role in the affairs of the state's only metropolitan center, making the university a more significant part of Arkansas's development. The University of Arkansas at Little Rock grew and flourished in the

1970s and 1980s. By becoming a tax-supported university with extensive graduate programs and bachelor's degree opportunities, it served a purpose far beyond that of the junior college founded by John Larson in 1927. In many respects, however, UALR remained the same basic institution as its forerunners — evolving and changing, but still serving the educational needs of the students of central Arkansas.

Appendix

Football Schedule--1949 LRJC Trojans Undefeated

State Teachers	Sept. 22	27-7
U. of A. freshmen	Oct. 1	34-0
St. Bernard	Oct. 8	46-7
Ouachita	Oct. 15	40-27
Monticello A&M	Oct. 22	39-25
Arkansas College	Oct. 28	70-12
College of the Ozarks	Nov. 5	34-13
Northeast Center	Nov. 12	50-13
McNeese	Nov. 25	33-7
Santa Ana, Calif.	Dec. 10	25-19

Recipients

of the Shield of the Trojan/Distinguished Alumnus Award
1950-1987

1950	Granville B. Davis	1985	Pat M. Riley
1951	William Darby	1986	Betty Fowler
1952	Mary Burt Nash	1987	Sam Bracy
1953	Robert Lowry		
1954	Jean Woolfolk		
1955	Bobbie Forster		
1956	Richard C. Butler		
1957	E. Grainger Williams		
1958	Windsor P. Booth		
1959	Drew Agar		
1960	James H. Rice		
1961	Matilda Tuohey		
1962	Robert Gannaway		
1963	Al Pollard		
1964	Lester G. McAllister		
1965	Fred Cloud		
1966	Roy Kumpe		
1967	Orville Henry		
1968	E. Lee McLean		
1969	Robert P. Taylor		
1970	Richard B. Dixon		
1971	Carlyle G. Caldwell		
1972	Harold J. Engstrom, Jr.		
1973	Alice Gray		
1974	Gerald Burns Robins		
1975	C.W. Koepple		
1976	Herschel H. Friday		
1977	John A. Larson		
1978	Claud L. Holbert		
1979	Peg Newton Smith		
1980	Alfred Kahn, Jr.		
1981	Frank L. Whitbeck		
1982	Jerry Maulden		
1983	Ben Allen, Jr.		
1984	Mary F. Worthen		

Notes

Introduction

1. Mary Best to George W. Donaghey, 8 July 1929.

2. Lawrence A. Kimpton, "The Junior College in America," *Junior College Journal*, February 1953, 303.

Chapter 1. Creating a People's College

1. Little Rock University, "A Study of Little Rock University: Its Origins, Present Program, and Future Plans" (Little Rock: November, 1959), 1.

2. *Arkansas Historical Quarterly*, Autumn 1944, 294.

3. J.H. Atkinson, "The Present Little Rock University: How It Began," *Pulaski County Historical Review*, March 1966, 6.

4. Interview with Pauline Hoeltzel, University of Arkansas at Little Rock Oral History Project, 1973, 13.

5. Charles R. Monroe, *Profile of the Community College* (San Francisco: Jossey-Bass, Inc., 1972), 5.

6. Ibid., 6.

7. Tommie J. Cole, "The Historical Development of Junior Colleges in Arkansas" (Ed.D. dissertation, University of Arkansas, Fayetteville, 1955), 12.

8. Monroe, 8.

9. Ibid.

10. Tyrus Hillway, *The American Two-year College* (New York: Harper and Company, 1958), 16.

11. Monroe, 11.

12. Ibid., 184.

13. Leland L. Medsker, *The Junior College: Progress and Prospect* (New York: McGraw-Hill,

1960), 20.

14. Hillway, 12.

15. Ibid., 7.

16. Ibid.

17. Cole, 17.

18. Hillway, vii.

19. Ibid.

20. Cole, 82.

21. Ibid., 76.

22. Ibid., 92.

23. Ibid., 115.

24. Ibid., 135.

25. *College Chatter*, 10 January 1935.

26. Atkinson, "Present LRU," 7.

27. Frances Ross and Anne Fulk, eds., *Grand Central: A Short History of Little Rock Central High School* (Little Rock: Central High School, 1983), 1. When Mrs. Lillian D. McDermott, president of the Little Rock School Board, signed the bonds for the school in 1924, she became the first woman ever to sign public construction bonds in excess of one million dollars.

28. Atkinson, "Present LRU," 8.

29. Ibid., 7.

30. Monroe, 356.

31. *Bulletin*, May 1930, 7.

32. Minutes of the Little Rock School Board, 30 August 1927.

Chapter 2. LRJC at Work and Play, 1927-1931

1. George W. Donaghey, *Autobiography* (Benton, Arkansas: L.B. White Printing Co., 1939), 311.

2. Waddy W. Moore, "George Washington Donaghey, 1909-1913," in *The Governors of Arkansas* (Fayetteville: University of Arkansas

222

Press, 1981), 129.
3. Ibid., 132.
4. M. LaFayette Harris to James H. Penick, 3 January 1946.
5. Donaghey, 308.
6. Ibid., 310.
7. *College Chatter*, 30 April 1946.
8. Ibid., 23 October 1929.
9. Atkinson, "Present LRU," 10.
10. *College Chatter*, 4 April 1935.
11. Ibid., 15 February 1933.
12. Ibid., 2 May 1945.
13. Ibid., 6 November 1929.
14. *Bulletin*, May 1930, 7.
15. Ibid.
16. *Trojan*, 1930, 34.
17. Hilda A. Elkins, "The John A. Larson Memorial Library, 1927-1960," 1.
18. Ibid., 2.
19. *College Chatter*, 2 May 1945.
20. Ibid.
21. Ibid., 30 October 1928.
22. Atkinson, "Present LRU," 9.
23. *Trojan*, 1930.
24. Ibid., 23.
25. *College Chatter*, 23 October 1929.
26. Ibid., 27 October 1949.
27. J.H. Atkinson, *LRU Chatter*, 27 November 1957.
28. *College Chatter*, 4 March 1929.
29. *Trojan*, 1931, 46.
30. *College Chatter*, 3 November 1933.
31. Ibid., 2 May 1945.
32. Ibid., 21 November 1929.
33. Atkinson, "Present LRU," 8.
34. *Bulletin*, May 1930, 8.
35. Hoeltzel, 4.

Chapter 3. Beginning Again, 1931-1935
1. Atkinson, "Present LRU," 8.
2. Minutes of the Little Rock School Board, 26 July 1930.
3. J.H. Atkinson, "LRJC: The First Ten Years, 1927-1937," *Pulaski County Historical Society Bulletin* No. 4, 1959, 13.
4. Ibid.
5. Minutes of the Little Rock School Board, 30 March 1931.
6. *College Chatter*, 4 September 1931.
7. Ibid.
8. Hoeltzel, 14.

9. *College Chatter*, 7 March 1934.
10. Hoeltzel, 14.
11. Minutes of the Little Rock School Board, 25 May 1934.
12. *Arkansas Gazette*, 25 February 1962.
13. Hugh Park, "James Harris Atkinson," *Arkansas Historical Quarterly*, Winter 1973, 371.
14. Ibid., 372.
15. *College Chatter*, 17 October 1938.
16. Ibid., 12 October 1950.
17. Atkinson, "LRJC," 17.
18. *Bulletin* 1932-33, 38.
19. Ibid., 1934-35, 11.
20. *College Chatter*, 4 September 1934.
21. *Bulletin* 1934-35, 12.
22. Elkins, 3.
23. *College Chatter*, 30 October 1939.
24. Hoeltzel, 6.
25. Atkinson, "LRJC," 22.
26. *College Chatter*, 5 December 1935.
27. Ibid., 18 October 1933.
28. Ibid., 10 October 1935.
29. Hoeltzel, 3.
30. Atkinson, "LRJC," 20.
31. *Trojan*, 1934.
32. Atkinson, "LRJC," 21.
33. *College Chatter*, 2 November 1934.
34. Atkinson, "LRJC," 15.
35. *College Chatter*, 1 May 1939.
36. Ibid., 2 December 1931.
37. Ibid,. 15 November 1934.
38. Ibid., 13 January 1932.
39. *Trojan*, 1935.
40. *College Chatter*, 21 March 1951.
41. Ibid., 17 April 1939.
42. Ibid., 23 March 1932.
43. Ibid., 2 May 1947.
44. Ibid., 23 October 1929.
45. Ibid., 27 January 1932.
46. Atkinson, "LRJC," 17.
47. *College Chatter*, 27 January 1932.
48. Ibid., 10 February 1932.

Chapter 4. The Peanut Butter College
1. *College Chatter*, 29 April 1941.
2. Ibid., 23 May 1938.
3. Minutes of the Little Rock Junior College Faculty Meeting, 11 September 1937.
4. Elkins, 9.
5. Ibid.
6. *College Chatter*, 22 April 1938.

7. Minutes of the Little Rock Junior College Faculty Meeting, 10 January 1939.
8. Monroe, 69.
9. Medsker, 56.
10. *College Chatter*, 17 April 1939.
11. Ibid., 14 January 1941.
12. Ibid., 27 November 1939.
13. "The Camera Oversees Life at LRJC," 8.
14. Minutes of the Little Rock School Board, 28 September 1937.
15. *College Chatter*, 3 November 1937.
16. Ibid., 7 November 1935.
17. Ibid., 30 October 1939.
18. Ibid., 20 May 1940.
19. Ibid., 15 December 1937.
20. Ibid., 24 January 1938.
21. Ibid., 13 November 1942.
22. Ibid., 5 November 1941.
23. Atkinson, "LRJC," 26.
24. *College Chatter*, 21 March 1935.
25. Minutes of the Little Rock School Board, 26 May 1935.
26. *College Chatter*, 9 April 1936.
27. Ibid., 6 October 1937.
28. Ibid., 5 November 1940.
29. Ibid., 4 April 1938.
30. Minutes of the Little Rock Junior College Faculty Meeting, 7 December 1936.
31. *Trojan*, 1938, 15.
32. *College Chatter*, 27 March 1939.
33. Minutes of the Little Rock Junior College Faculty Meeting, 21 March 1939.
34. *College Chatter*, 9 April 1945.
35. Ibid., 22 September 1936.
36. Ibid., 22 April 1938.
37. Ibid., 27 November 1939.
38. Hillway, 84.
39. *College Chatter*, 30 March 1944.
40. Medsker, 30.
41. Hillway, 84.
42. *College Chatter*, 22 April 1954.
43. Hoeltzel, 12.
44. *College Chatter*, 22 September 1936.
45. *Trojan*, 1938, 43.
46. *College Chatter*, 14 November 1938.
47. Ibid., 30 January 1935.
48. Ibid., 12 February 1940.
49. Ibid., 7 April 1937.
50. Ibid.
51. Ibid., 26 February 1940.

Chapter 5. From Pearl Harbor to Hayes Street, 1941-1949
1. *College Chatter*, 17 December 1941.
2. Ibid., 2 May 1945.
3. Ibid., 24 September 1941.
4. Elkins, 14.
5. *College Chatter*, 24 September 1941.
6. Ibid., 29 October 1942.
7. Ibid., 20 May 1942.
8. Minutes of the Little Rock Junior College Faculty Meeting, 13 January 1943.
9. Ibid., December 1941.
10. Ibid., 12 September 1942.
11. *College Chatter*, 30 September 1942.
12. Ibid., 9 March 1944.
13. Ibid., 25 February 1943.
14. Ibid., 23 March 1945.
15. Ibid., 9 March 1944.
16. Ibid., 3 February 1944.
17. Ibid., 11 February 1943.
18. Ibid., 11 March 1943.
19. Ibid., 13 November 1942.
20. Ibid., 6 October 1943.
21. *Trojan*, 1947.
22. *College Chatter*, 8 October 1953.
23. Ibid., 27 September 1946.
24. Ibid., 11 October 1946.
25. Ibid., 11 February 1947.
26. Hoeltzel, 7.
27. E.Q. Brothers to the Little Rock School Board, 13 April 1950.
28. Undated memo, UALR Archives.
29. Memo, 17 January 1947.
30. Undated memo, UALR Archives.
31. Ibid.
32. M. LaFayette Harris to James H. Penick, 3 January 1946.
33. Ibid.
34. James H. Penick to M. LaFayette Harris, 22 January 1946.
35. James H. Penick to M.S. Davage, 28 January 1946.
36. Joe H. Bilheimer to the Little Rock School Board, 9 July 1948.
37. Hoeltzel, 8.
38. *College Chatter*, 16 May 1947.
39. James H. Penick, "Speech to the Supporters of the Permanent Home Campaign," undated, UALR Archives.
40. "LRJC — The First 25 Years, 1927-1952," 1.
41. *College Chatter*, 4 February 1948.
42. Untitled Permanent Home Campaign pamphlet.

43. "James H. Penick to Prominent County Leaders," undated, UALR Archives.
44. A.G. Kahn to J.H. Penick, 2 February 1948.
45. Arthur E. McLean to the Shareholders of the Commercial National Bank, 22 January 1948.
46. William A. McDonnell to James H. Penick, undated, UALR Archives.
47. *Arkansas Gazette*, 20 July 1952.
48. Minutes of the Little Rock Junior College Faculty Meeting, 3 March 1952.
49. J.A. Larson to the Little Rock School Board, 26 June 1947.
50. *College Chatter*, 1 December 1949.
51. Ibid.
52. Ibid.
53. Ibid., 14 May 1950.

Chapter 6. Student Life in the Golden Age, 1947-1957

1. "Report to the North Central Association of Colleges and Secondary Schools," 1954.
2. President's Report, 1956-57.
3. *College Chatter*, 19 October 1956.
4. Ibid., 27 September 1946.
5. Ibid., 11 February 1947.
6. Ibid., 2 April 1947.
7. Ibid., 2 May 1947.
8. Interview with Jimmy Karam, University of Arkansas at Little Rock Oral History Project, 1977, 1.
9. Ibid., 3.
10. *College Chatter*, 10 November 1949.
11. Ibid., 8 March 1948.
12. Ibid., 20 October 1948.
13. Ibid., 29 September 1949.
14. Ibid., 27 October 1949.
15. Ibid., 10 November 1949.
16. Ibid., 1 December 1949.
17. *Arkansas Democrat*, 21 November 1949.
18. *College Chatter*, 21 December 1949.
19. Memo to the Board of Trustees, 22 February 1951.
20. Karam, 4.
21. Tom Williams to Foster Vineyard, 28 March 1953.
22. Karam, 6.
23. *Arkansas Gazette*, 2 February 1986.
24. *College Chatter*, 6 May 1948.
25. J.A. Larson to Manning M. Pattillo, 24 September 1949.
26. Manning M. Pattillo to J.A. Larson, 29 September 1949.
27. Minutes of the Little Rock School Board, February 1950.
28. *College Chatter*, 23 February 1950.
29. *Trojan*, 1953.
30. Ibid.
31. *College Chatter*, 22 April 1954.
32. Ibid., 1 April 1946.
33. Ibid., 8 April 1954.
34. Minutes of the Little Rock Junior College Faculty Meeting, 1 February 1950.
35. *College Chatter*, 22 April 1954.
36. Ibid., 24 March 1955.
37. Ibid., 6 October 1948.
38. Ibid., 17 January 1947.
39. Ibid., 25 October 1951.
40. Ibid., 23 February 1950.
41. Minutes of the Little Rock Junior College Faculty Meeting, October 1951.
42. President's Report, 1956-57.
43. *Alumni News Letter*, June 1955.
44. *College Chatter*, 29 October 1942.

Chapter 7. Under New Leadership

1. *Alumni News Letter*, October 1952.
2. *College Chatter*, 21 December 1949.
3. Ibid., 29 September 1950.
4. Minutes of the Little Rock Junior College Faculty Meeting, 27 May 1948.
5. *Trojan*, 1951.
6. Ottenheimer Report, 1956, 20.
7. President's Report, 1956-57.
8. Ottenheimer, 19.
9. Ibid.
10. *College Chatter*, 18 November 1954.
11. Ibid, 22.
12. President's Report, 1956-57.
13. Ottenheimer, 21.
14. E.Q. Brothers to the Little Rock School Board, 9 February 1950.
15. *College Chatter*, 9 January 1939.
16. E.Q. Brothers to the Little Rock School Board, 15 June 1950.
17. *College Chatter*, 6 May 1948.
18. Granville D. Davis to the Board of Trustees, 16 April 1951.
19. Little Rock Junior College *Catalogue*, 1949-50, 4.
20. Meeting of the Little Rock Junior College Faculty, 27 March 1953.

21. Ibid., 12 April 1950.
22. Granville D. Davis to John Osman, 24 Febraury 1954.
23. President's Report, 1956-57.
24. Hillway, 31.
25. "Memo to the Board of Trustees," 25 January 1951.
26. *Arkansas Gazette*, 20 July 1952.
27. "Memo to the Board of Trustees," 31 May 1951.
28. Ibid., 27 September 1951.
29. Foster Vineyard to E.Q. Brothers and members of the Board of Trustees of Little Rock Junior College, 11 November 1954.
30. John Osman to Foster Vineyard, 29 November 1954.
31. "Notes on a Statement made by Dr. Osman," undated.
32. Elkins, 18.
33. "Memo," September 1954.
34. Ottenheimer, 24.
35. *College Chatter*, 4 September 1952.
36. Granville D. Davis to the Board of Trustees, 31 July 1952.
37. Charles Pyles to Andy Ritger, 16 June 1952.
38. *College Chatter*, 17 January 1952.
39. Granville Davis to the Director of Athletics, Tyler Junior College, 14 August 1952.
40. Meeting of the Little Rock Junior College Faculty, 15 April 1952.
41. *College Chatter*, 8 February 1951.
42. Charles B. Pyles to Treasurer, Tougaloo College, 22 October 1952.
43. *College Chatter*, 19 November 1947.

Chapter 8. Toward a Municipal University

1. Quoted in *Arkansas Gazette*, 3 July 1954.
2. *College Chatter*, 14 December 1932.
3. Ibid., 14 January 1941.
4. Ibid., 11 October 1946.
5. Earl W. Anderson, "Report of Evaluation of Little Rock Junior College in Terms of Possibilities of Expanding into a Four-year College," 1.
6. *Arkansas Gazette*, 3 July 1954.
7. Granville D. Davis to John T. Caldwell, 29 August 1953.
8. John T. Caldwell to Granville D. Davis, 10 September 1953.
9. John T. Caldwell to Granville D. Davis, 13 August 1953.
10. *College Chatter*, 25 November 1953.
11. Quoted in *Little Rock Junior College vs. the George W. Donaghey Foundation*, Supreme Court of the State of Arkansas, "Brief for the Appellees," 11.
12. Trustees of the George W. Donaghey Foundation, "Resolution," 9 June 1954.
13. *LRJC vs. Donaghey Foundation*, 80.
14. A.L. Barber to the Trustees of the G.W. Donaghey Foundation, 8 June 1954.
15. *Alumni News Letter*, October 1954.
16. *College Chatter*, 16 June 1936.
17. *LRJC vs. Donaghey Foundation*, 10.
18. Granville D. Davis to James H. Penick, 21 July 1952.
19. *Arkansas Gazette*, 3 July 1954.
20. Ibid., 4 July 1954.
21. Ibid., 15 May 1955.
22. Ibid., 6 July 1954.
23. Roger H. Howard to Charles L. Thompson, 6 July 1954.
24. Paul S. Rippier to Leo Pfeifer, 5 July 1954.
25. *Arkansas Gazette*, 19 August 1954.
26. Granville D. Davis, "Resignation Statement," 7 July 1954.
27. Ibid.
28. Interview with Carey V. Stabler, University of Arkansas at Little Rock Oral History Project, 1977.
29. Ira Corn to the Editor of the *Arkansas Gazette*, 23 July 1954.
30. *LRJC vs. Donaghey Foundation*, 13.
31. *Arkansas Gazette*, 5 October 1954.
32. *Alumni News Letter*, June 1955.
33. Ottenheimer, 2.
34. Ibid., 27.
35. Ibid., 5.
36. Ibid., 4.
37. Ibid., 24.
38. Ibid., 38.
39. *Arkansas Gazette*, 13 May 1956.
40. Ottenheimer, 7.
41. Ibid., 9.
42. Ibid., 4.
43. Statement of the Trustees of the George W. Donaghey Foundation, 15 May 1956.
44. *College Chatter*, 27 September 1956.
45. Stabler, 1.

Chapter 9. Whatever Happened to Donaghey College?

1. *College Chatter*, 1 February 1957.
2. Ibid., 19 October 1956.
3. Minutes of the Little Rock Junior College Board, 20 December 1956.
4. Ottenheimer, 25.
5. Minutes of the Little Rock Junior College Board, 25 September 1956.
6. Wayne Upton to Carey V. Stabler, 17 April 1957.
7. Most Reverend Albert L. Fletcher to W.G. Cooper, 1 March 1957.
8. Minutes of the Little Rock Junior College Board, 22 February 1957.
9. Ibid., 30 May 1957.
10. *LRU Chatter*, 6 February 1958.
11. "Greater Little Rock Needs a Senior College," 1956.
12. Letter to Campaign Workers, 9 January 1957.
13. *College Chatter*, 22 March 1957.
14. John H. Rule to R.D. Lowry, 11 January 1957.
15. Stabler, 6.
16. President's Report, 1956-57.
17. John H. Rule to Dr. Irwin J. Lubbers, 20 January 1960.
18. *Campus Bulletin*, 28 April 1986.
19. President's Report, 1956-57.
20. Minutes of the Little Rock University Board of Trustees, 15 June 1960.
21. Irwin J. Lubbers, "Report of an Accrediting Examination of Little Rock University," 14-15 December 1959, 6.
22. President's Report, 1956-57.
23. Ottenheimer, 19.
24. *Arkansas Gazette*, 22 March 1959.
25. *Arkansas Democrat*, 28 September 1959.
26. *LRU Chatter*, 13 February 1959.
27. *Alumni News Letter*, May 1962.
28. *Arkansas Democrat*, 13 August 1957.
29. Minutes of the Little Rock University Board of Trustees Meeting, 26 October 1960.
30. Ibid., 29 April 1964.
31. President's Report, 1958-59.
32. Jeanne E. Cook to Carey V. Stabler, 20 May 1961.
33. Irwin J. Lubbers, "Report of an Accrediting Examination of Little Rock University," 14-15 December 1959, 4.
34. Annual Report of the Dean of the University, 1 July 1960.
35. Stabler, 20.
36. Minutes of the Little Rock University Board of Trustees Meeting, 28 January 1959.
37. *George W. Donaghey Foundation vs. Little Rock University*, Supreme Court of the State of Arkansas, 1960.
38. Ibid.
39. Ibid.
40. Stabler, 17.
41. John Forbes to Carey V. Stabler, 6 April 1960.
42. *Arkansas Gazette*, 2 April 1960.
43. Irwin J. Lubbers to Carey V. Stabler, 13 May 1960.
44. Hoeltzel, 16.
45. Ibid.
46. H. Tyndall Dickinson to Carey V. Stabler, 8 June 1961.
47. *Campus Bulletin*.
48. Carey Stabler, "Report to the Board of Trustees," 23 May 1962.

Chapter 10. "A Song That's Ever New," 1957-1963

1. Irwin J. Lubbers, "Report," 6.
2. Ibid.
3. C.W. Kreger to Carey V. Stabler, 4 April 1958.
4. President's Report, 1956-57.
5. Ibid., 15 June 1960.
6. Stabler, 9.
7. Carey Stabler to E. Grainger Williams, June 1961.
8. Annual Report of the Dean.
9. *Arkansas Gazette*, 4 September 1960.
10. *Bulletin* 1962-63, 106.
11. *Arkansas Gazette*, 21 January 1962.
12. Ibid., 15 July 1958.
13. Minutes of the Meeting of the Little Rock University Faculty, 2 May 1958.
14. *LRU Chatter*, 2 October 1958.
15. Minutes of the Meeting of the Little Rock University Faculty, 1 April 1959.
16. Ibid., 29 September 1958.
17. Robert F. Sullivan to Carey Stabler, 5 July 1963.
18. J.R. Leeds to Carey V. Stabler, 21 July 1959.
19. *Arkansas Democrat*, 1 September 1957.
20. Ibid., 15 December 1957.
21. Stabler, 9.

22. *Arkansas Gazette*, 15 April 1957.
23. *Arkansas Democrat*, 7 January 1962.
24. N.W. Quick to R.C. Cox, 6 January 1958.
25. *Arkansas Gazette*, 8 December 1957.
26. Minutes of the Board of Trustees of Little Rock University, 4 March 1958.
27. President's Report, 1956-57.
28. *Forum*, 19 April 1963.
29. Minutes of the Board of Trustees of Little Rock University, 28 January 1959.
30. Hoeltzel, 17.
31. Minutes of the Board of Trustees of Little Rock University, 10 August 1964.
32. Carey V. Stabler to Charles G. Moss, 31 August 1964.
33. Carey V. Stabler to Earl J. McGrath, 9 September 1964.
34. President's Report, October 1960.
35. Carey V. Stabler to E. Grainger Williams, 9 February 1962.
36. *Forum*, 4 October 1962.
37. D.S. Beard to Carey Stabler, 3 December 1962.
38. *Arkansas Gazette*, 10 March 1960.
39. *LRU Chatter*, 20 May 1958.
40. *Forum*, 21 April 1961.
41. Confidential communication, 10 May 1986.
42. Minutes of the Meeting of the Little Rock University Faculty, 3 April 1963.
43. *Bulletin* 1962-63.
44. Annual Report of the Dean.
45. Carey V. Stabler to Grainger Williams, 13 September 1961.
46. Minutes of the Meeting of the Little Rock University Faculty, 7 February 1962.
47. President's Report, November 1961.
48. *Forum*, 1 February 1967.
49. Ervin L. Betts to Kent Ingram, 2 December 1964.
50. Everett L. Edmondson to Ervin L. Betts, 24 November 1964.
51. Minutes of the Board of Trustees of Little Rock University, 31 May 1960.
52. President's Report, 31 May 1960.
53. *Arkansas Gazette*, 21 March 1962.
54. President's Report, November 1961.

Chapter 11. "Last Resort University"
1. *Forum*, 28 February 1963.
2. President's Report, 27 November 1968.
3. *Arkansas Democrat*, 7 December 1963.
4. *Arkansas Gazette*, 6 May 1964.
5. *Forum*, 23 January 1964.
6. Stabler, 22.
7. *North Little Rock Times*, 9 April 1964.
8. *Forum*, 18 November 1965.
9. President's Report, 28 October 1964.
10. Ibid., February 1967.
11. Stabler, 10.
12. President's Report, 14 April 1969.
13. *Arkansas Gazette*, 17 January 1965.
14. Stabler, 10.
15. *Arkansas Democrat*, 30 May 1967.
16. Minutes of the Academic Affairs Committee, April 1968.
17. President's Report, 1967-69.
18. *Forum*, 18 November 1965.
19. President's Report, 26 February 1969.
20. *Bulletin* 1965-66.
21. Tom Williams to Foster Vineyard, 28 March 1953.
22. *LRU Chatter*, 2 October 1958.
23. *Forum*, 17 April 1964.
24. Minutes of the Board of Trustees of Little Rock University, 30 August 1960.
25. *Bulletin* 1965-66, 4.
26. Stabler, 19.
27. Tom Broce to Carey V. Stabler, 6 October 1961.
28. Ibid.
29. "Notes on Conference on Recruiting," undated, University of Arkansas at Little Rock Archives.
30. Harold I. Woolard to Carey V. Stabler, 14 September 1961.
31. "Mean Scores on the Graduate Record Exam," 1962.
32. President's Report, September 1958.
33. *Arkansas Gazette*, 15 May 1966.
34. Ibid., 5 April 1966.
35. Ibid., 10 June 1984.
36. Jerry D. Corley to the Reverend J.R. Phillips, 9 May 1967.
37. *Arkansas Gazette*, 26 July 1967.
38. *Arkansas Democrat*, 23 February 1966.
39. *Arkansas Gazette*, 21 October 1969.
40. President's Report, March 1967.
41. "Petition to the Student Senate," Spring 1969.
42. "A Document Petitioning the Student Senate of Little Rock University," undated, University of Arkansas at Little Rock Archives.
43. President's Report, 26 March 1969.

44. *Arkansas Gazette*, 1 October 1969.

Chapter 12. Merger
1. *Trojan*, 1962.
2. Interview with Dr. James Fribrough, 9 July 1986.
3. *Forum*, 13 January 1966.
4. Walter S. McNutt, *A History of Arkansas* (Little Rock: The Arkansas House, 1932), 551.
5. John Ferguson and J.H. Atkinson, *Historic Arkansas* (Little Rock: The Arkansas History Commission, 1966), 290.
6. Ottenheimer, 10.
7. *Arkansas Democrat*, 23 May 1956.
8. *Arkansas Gazette*, 2 February 1986.
9. Lloyd W. Bowie to Everette Edmondson, 19 November 1964.
10. Karl H. Dannenfeldt, "A Report on the Visit by a Consultant of the North Central Association to Little Rock University," 17-19 April 1966.
11. Fribrough.
12. David W. Mullins to the Board of Trustees of the University of Arkansas, 16 June 1966.
13. Minutes of the Advisory Council, 9 May 1968.
14. *Arkansas Gazette*, 13 January 1969.
15. Robert A. Leflar, *The First 100 Years: Centennial History of the University of Arkansas*, (Fayetteville: University of Arkansas Foundation, Inc.), 1972, 210.
16. *North Little Rock Times*, 23 June 1966.
17. David W. Mullins to the Board of Trustees of the University of Arkansas, 16 June 1966.
18. *Arkansas Gazette*, 17 June 1966.
19. Ibid.
20. President's Report, March 1966.
21. Fribrough.
22. Stabler, 13.
23. Ibid.
24. President's Report, September 1966.
25. *Forum*, 14 September 1966.
26. Ibid., 10 October 1966.
27. *Arkansas Gazette*, 1 October 1966.
28. Ibid., 17 December 1966.
29. Ibid., 20 January 1967.
30. *Forum*, 1 February 1967.
31. Hot Springs *Sentinel-Record*, 16 July 1967.
32. *Log Cabin Democrat*, 8 August 1967.
33. *Arkansas Gazette*, 4 October 1967.
34. Leflar, 210.
35. *Arkansas Gazette*, 30 January 1969.
36. Ibid., 10 April 1969.
37. Leflar, 214.
38. Carey V. Stabler to Wayne Upton, 9 August 1967.
39. Stabler, 14.
40. *North Little Rock Times*, 13 July 1967.

Bibliographic Essay

The majority of material used in the preparation of *The People's College: Little Rock Junior College and Little Rock University, 1927-1969* is located in the archives of the Ottenheimer Library at the University of Arkansas at Little Rock. Under the direction of head archivist Dr. Bobby Roberts, the archival staff has assembled and processed a comprehensive collection of documents relating to the history of the college from the founding of the school in 1927 until the merger with the University of Arkansas in 1969.

The collection includes an almost complete set of material published by the institution during the Little Rock Junior College and Little Rock University eras. One of the most valuable sources for the researcher in this regard is the campus newspaper, the *College Chatter*, which became the *LRU Chatter* before assuming the name the *Forum* after the school became a four-year institution in 1957. The back issues of the paper offer many profiles of campus personalities; detailed chronicles of sports events, the arrivals and departures of faculty members, and activities; and student opinion on a variety of topics. Unfortunately, the UALR archival collection does not include issues of the *Forum* between the years 1967 and 1969. Other important sources

that originated at the college are the *Trojan*, the pictorial yearbook; the *Bulletins* of the institution, which lists all rules and regulations as well as courses offered by Jaycee or LRU; and the *Alumni News Letter*, which the school distributed in the late 1940s and early 1950s to keep the junior college alumni abreast of both campus events and alumni activities.

The UALR archives also include a wealth of primary material detailing the daily operations of the institution. One source that proved to be of particular help in the writing of this manuscript was the annual President's Report to the Board of Trustees. These documents often summarize highlights of the past year at the college and discuss economic and other problems facing the institution in the upcoming year. The minutes of the faculty meetings and meetings of the board of trustees usually involve only a prefunctory treatment of issues, omitting disagreement or debate on important matters. In contrast, the collection of letters and memos — both to and from individuals inside and outside of the college community — contains a wealth of information and candid opinions of numerous aspects of the development of the junior college and the university. In addition, reports by consultants like Earl W. Anderson and C.W. Kreger also contain candid material on some of the college's deficiencies and difficulties at various stages of the school's growth.

Another valuable source is a set of self-studies written by the school's instructional staff in preparation for the accreditation examinations conducted by the North Central Association of Colleges and Secondary Schools. By far the most comprehensive of these studies, and an excellent source of statistical and other information on the institution, is "A Study of Little Rock University: Its Origins, Present Program, and Future Plans" (Little Rock: November 1959). The UALR archives also house an incomplete set of files from the Donaghey Foundation.

Some of the most important sources for the study of the history of an institution are the memories and observations of the people who worked for the organization over the years. J.H. Atkinson, a historian who taught at Little Rock Junior College from the school's inception in 1927 until his retirement in 1957 wrote two articles on Jaycee's early years — "Little Rock Junior College: The First Ten Years, 1927-1937" (*Pulaski County Historical Society Bulletin* 4, 1959) and "The Present Little Rock University: How It Began" (*Pulaski County Historical Review*, March, 1966). Hilda A. Elkins, who worked in the college library, authored a brief unpublished history of the facility entitled "The John A. Larson Memorial Library, 1927-1960." In the 1970s the UALR Oral History Project conducted a series of interviews with Pauline Hoeltzel, a longtime faculty member; Jimmy Karam, the coach of LRJC's 1949 championship football team;

and Dr. Carey V. Stabler, the president of the school during the LRU years. The transcripts of these interviews provide many valuable insights into the operation of the institution at various stages of its development, as does an extensive interview with Dr. James Fribourgh, a teacher and administrator at the college for almost 40 years, conducted by the author. Other important primary material includes the report of the Ottenheimer Committee, a citizens' task force, whose survey in 1955 directly led to the transition from Little Rock Junior College to Little Rock University. George W. Donaghey's *Autobiography* (Benton, Arkansas: L.B. White Printing Company, 1939) offers explanations of why the ex-governor decided to endow the struggling junior college in 1927. Newspaper accounts also offer an invaluable record of events in the life of an institution, and articles from the *Arkansas Gazette*, *Arkansas Democrat*, and *North Little Rock Times*, preserved on microfilm or in scrapbooks, offer such a chronicle in the case of LRJC and LRU.

Although most sources for *The People's College* are located in the UALR archives, material such as the minutes of the meetings of the Little Rock School Board, generously made available by the staff of the Little Rock School District, and the records of the Supreme Court of Arkansas also contain worthwhile information. Along with the considerable primary material on the history of the college, several secondary works add to an understanding of the development of the institution. On the subject of the junior college movement in America, Charles R. Monroe's *Profile of the Community College* (San Francisco: Jossey-Bass, Inc., 1972); Tyrus Hillway's *The American*

Two-Year College (New York: Harper and Row, 1958); and Leland L. Medsker's *The Junior College: Progress and Prospect* (New York: McGraw-Hill, 1960), were especially valuable — although a more recent historical narrative of the movement, concentrating on the overall significance of the subject, would be a valuable addition to the literature on higher education in the United States. Robert L. Kennedy's "The Economic Impact of Higher Education in Arkansas" (Ph.D. dissertation, University of Missouri-Columbia, 1984) and Tommie J. Cole's "The Historical Development of Junior Colleges in Arkansas" (Ed.D. dissertation, University of Arkansas, 1955) both contain excellent material on the history of higher education in Arkansas. In addition, the following books provide background information on the state's history: Timothy P. Donovan and Willard B. Gatewood, Jr. (editors), *The Governors of Arkansas* (Fayetteville: University of Arkansas Press, 1981); Walter S. McNutt, *A History of Arkansas* (Little Rock: The Arkansas House, 1932); John Ferguson and J.H. Atkinson, *Historic Arkansas* (Little Rock: Arkansas History Commission, 1966); and James W. Bell, *Little Rock Handbook* (Little Rock: Publishers Bookshop, Inc., 1980). For historical information on the University of Arkansas, Robert A. Leflar's *The First 100 Years: Centennial History of the University of Arkansas* (Fayetteville: University of Arkansas Foundation, Inc., 1972) updates earlier studies by John Hugh Reynolds and David Y. Thomas in 1910 and Harrison Hale in 1948.

Index